Boocoo Dinky Dow

My short, crazy Vietnam War

By Grady C. Myers
and Julie Titone

Copyright © 2012 Julie Titone

All rights reserved.

ISBN: 146795568X

ISBN-13: 978-1467955683

Dedicated to the men of Charlie Company and their families,

including Jake, Megan, John and Kevin Myers.

Illustrations by Grady C. Myers. "Toymaker," "Still Life with Combat Infantry Badge," "Mascot," and "Seventeen Months, Twenty-Nine Days" are from the collection of the National Veterans Art Museum.

Special thanks to editors Ross Carletta and Richard Harlan Miller.

Author's note

This book is history, not fiction. But it is just one man's history, based on his memories of a chaotic time, and the men who knew Grady Myers as "Hoss" have their own and sometimes differing recollections of these events. Those veterans—and all other readers—are welcome to share their stories and reactions in the "Memo to Charlie Company" blog online at shortcrazyvietnam.com.

Preface ... Page 1

Chapter 1: In country ... Page 4

Chapter 2: Mocking fate ... Page 8

Chapter 3: A dubious honor ... Page 13

Chapter 4: The worst that ever happened ... Page 25

Chapter 5: Changing fortunes ... Page 36

Chapter 6: Kill those commies ... Page 52

Chapter 7: Assembly line to Vietnam ... Page 54

Chapter 8: Anywhere but the 4th ... Page 59

Chapter 9: Moving out ... Page 64

Chapter 10: Dak To days ... Page 68

Chapter 11: *Beaucoup dien cai dau* ... Page 74

Chapter 12: Combustion Charlie ... Page 105

Chapter 13: Rosemary's Baby and the traffic Gestapo ... Page 116

Chapter 14: Stiletto ... Page 121

Chapter 15: The bowels of hell ... Page 125

Chapter 16: Ambush ... Page 136

Chapter 17: Travelogue of the wounded ... Page 144

Chapter 18: Fitzsimmons ... Page 151

Chapter 19: Stay out ... Page 161

Epilogue ... Page 162

Preface

In the late 1970s, Grady Myers was an artist at the Boise, Idaho, newspaper. I was a young features editor. When we went separately to an office party where people were supposed to dress like they did in the '60s, my costume was a giant 45 rpm record. Grady wore fatigues and told entertaining stories about serving in the Vietnam War. I was fascinated. In those days, the military used a lottery system to draft young men. Most guys I grew up with had college deferments or high draft lottery numbers, and managed to avoid Vietnam. If they'd gone, they rarely talked about it.

I asked Grady if I could write down his stories. He said yes. I stocked the fridge with Old Milwaukee, bought a cassette recorder and got him talking.

When I transcribed the tapes, I thought: This is like "M*A*S*H," only set in Vietnam instead of Korea. Of course, not all of Grady's stories involved humor, even black humor. People died. People suffered. He suffered. But Grady recounted even the saddest parts as if telling an adventure story. His descriptions were those of an artist and a reporter: detailed and full of sights, sounds, smells.

To put the interviews in context, I learned more about what the Vietnamese called the American War. Grady had been "in-country" for a few months in 1968-'69, at the war's height, when the U.S. had half a million troops in Vietnam. Desperate to keep the troop pipeline filled, the Army was taking people with physical and mental shortcomings who would normally have been unacceptable. That included Grady, an extremely nearsighted 19-year-old.

Grady and I produced a manuscript that I typed on an electric Smith Corona and he illustrated with drawings. We also produced a marriage, a son, a divorce and an enduring friendship. The manuscript stayed in a series of closets and packing boxes.

When Grady was in his late 50s, he began thinking about the war a lot, thanks to information he found on the Internet. He learned things he'd never known, including that he had participated in a military operation dubbed Wayne Grey. After decades of separation from his Army buddies, who knew him as "Hoss," he discovered that Charlie Company had started to hold reunions. He was never able to attend.

Health problems had confined Grady to a wheelchair and, eventually, to a nursing home bed. He needed something to occupy his mind. So we dusted off the book manuscript. He propped himself up so he could see his computer and created new artwork, this time collages made from Vietnam photos he discovered online. He painstakingly reviewed the manuscript, adding details. He added more profanity, too, because that's the way the soldiers talked. When I deleted some cuss words with the argument that they interfered with the narrative flow, his reaction was a grudging OK, so long as I didn't girl-ify the story with "heck" and "darn."

The names and nicknames in this memoir are real insofar as Grady could remember them, except for Phillips, Oates, Shadow and Stiletto. Grady made up those names because he didn't recall, or never knew, the real ones. Soldiers in Vietnam didn't learn the names of everyone who came and went during their tours of duty. Sometimes, given the chance a newcomer would die, they didn't want to get that close.

Names aside, Grady vividly remembered many experiences in Vietnam. The emotions stuck to his brain like the red tropical dirt stuck to his body. He called it a time of intensive living. He told his wartime stories—always complete with sound effects (his helicopter imitation was second to none)—without rancor or regret. He did sometimes come down hard on himself. After he'd reviewed his behavior as described near the end of this book, he e-mailed me to say, "I'm finding I don't like Spec. Myers very much." I replied that I liked the young soldier a whole lot. He was so ... human.

Grady was a man of contrasts. Big talent, small ego. Strong language, gentle spirit. His tough constitution was legendary, as was the disregard he showed for his health. A futile war left him in pain, yet he was proud of his military service. He was well-acquainted with depression, yet all of his life he made people laugh.

He once looked at a picture of himself in Vietnam, in which his camouflaged helmet accentuated his strong jaw and big eyeglasses.

"I was just a kid," he said. "Hell, we were all just kids."

Now, Grady's kids have kids. When he died, I thought it was time to share his stories.

Julie Titone
Spring, 2012

Firebase Below

Chapter 1: In country

I wasn't sure what gripped my gut harder: the lifting sensation of my first helicopter ride or the anticipation of my first assignment as a "grunt" at the front. Or what passed for front lines in a war in which the enemy seemed to be everywhere.

When the roaring olive elevator had risen above its cloud of dust, I looked down on Dak To, the dirty, battered camp that had been home for three days. Then the Huey dipped its nose and followed the path of a river. For 20 minutes, its shadow darted like a bug between the snaking brown water and the emerald vegetation that crowded the riverbanks.

The chopper veered to a green cone of a hill. The top of the cone was shaved and dotted with sandbagged wooden structures. It looked like crates had been nailed to the top of a gigantic, pointed, bald head. An undefined glittering circled the baldness, rising through the heat like a halo.

That unlikely pinnacle was Fire Support Base 30.

The helipad was a reasonably flat area scooped out of the hillside.

When our chopper landed, I jumped out, along with two other replacements, Medford and Johnson. A shirtless but helmeted crowd lunged in under the spinning blades like a NASCAR pit crew and began yanking bags and boxes off the vibrating aircraft. We grabbed our gear, extra ammo and supplies that the crew chief shoved after us, and marched up the trail through the area that had glittered at us from the air. Up close, it looked like the official dump of the Vietnam War.

There were bullet-riddled pieces of helicopters, charred helmets, ammunition casings, glass fragments and tin cans among the paper trash that covered the ground and hung on the barbed wire. Whenever a soldier took out the trash, he sure as hell wasn't going to walk into the jungle and risk getting shot or tripping a flare just to be Mr. Clean. Instead, he'd stand in the perimeter trench and toss his trash.

The fact that the trash dissipated at the top of the hill only made the fire base less interesting, not less bleak. The midmorning sun didn't dispel the dinginess of the sandbag-stacked bunkers, the tarp-covered hooches pounded together out of scrap lumber and sandbags, the socks and shirts strewn about to dry. Everything was blanketed with red dirt. Reddish brown was the prevailing color; smoky diesel fuel burning in cut-down oil drums of shit provided the prevailing smell.

"Look at the pukes," someone yelled at us. "Catch the smell of fresh fish!"

At six-foot-five, I dwarfed the other newcomers, the tall beanpole Johnson and the little guy, Medford.

"Look at the big FNG, Sarge."

The fucking new guy was me.

Two platoon sergeants rushed alongside me, muttered "Jesus Christ" in unison and beat the trio to the command hooch. When Medford, Johnson and I arrived there, they were pleading with the company exec.

"We want him sir, we want the big one. Jesus fuckin' Christ, we gotta have him, sir."

"Look, he and the little one are already slated to go to somebody else, so quit bugging me," the exec said. He scowled and turned his attention to the fresh fish. "Glad to see you guys here. Goddamn, we're glad to see more people here."

The sergeants, issuing profanities at their profound loss of my burly ass, turned to leave. One of them shook his head. "Boy, you're a big one. You're gonna be hump'n' the 'Big Pig,' our new platoon M-60."

The M-60 was 23 pounds of machine gun, the biggest tool in a squad's shed. It made its handler a favorite enemy target. I was afraid of humping one.

The 2nd platoon leader was gone, back to battalion, the exec said. So was the company commander, who was in Hawaii on R&R. So was the platoon sergeant, who was at the rear buying beer. It was December 23, 1968, and the men had pooled their money to buy ample refreshments for their Christmas celebration.

We got our orders, despite the shortage of higher-ups to give them. Johnson was going to the first platoon, on the other side of the hill from the second platoon, where Medford and I were sent. At the end of the trail, which at points was made only of slats bridging bunker-tops, our squad leader greeted us. He was blond and blue-eyed and named Steve Stotka.

Buck Sgt. Stotka was the Midwestern football player he looked to be.

"Hi, how are you guys?" he demanded as much as asked, standing there with his muscular arm outstretched. After all of those numbing, boring days at the rear, I could hardly believe I was actually on the line, in the war. And here strutted this junior, tow-headed John Wayne wannabe who probably planned to have this little fracas whipped in time to get back for the next fall hunting season.

"I'll talk to you guys individually," Stotka said. Off he went with Medford.

In fifteen minutes, Stotka was back, and had me drop my gear outside his bunker, the squad leader's hooch. "Come with me. Let's find out about each other a little bit."

The two of us—one 19, the other two years older and vastly wiser, thanks to three months of NCO schooling in the art of leading men — sat on the edge of a bunker looking over the perimeter at the jungle, feet dangling, like school kids talking at a riverside.

"One of the first things we've got to get out of the way, Myers, is your needing a nickname," Stotka said.

"I really don't want a nickname. Isn't 'Grady' good enough?"

"Nope, nope, you've gotta have a nickname. Let's see here, uh …. Didn't you have a nickname when you were in basic? Big guys like you always get a nickname, don't they?"

"Yeah. They called me Teenie."

"Nah, that won't do. Did you get one back in high school?"

"Yeah. They called me Rosie O'Grady."

"That's no fucking good, either. Let's call ya Hoss. Whenever I holler, 'Hoss,' you come running. OK?"

"OK."

Then Stotka started in on the whole "Ya gotta love being in the Army" pitch, which I hadn't heard since way back in basic training.

"We're a hard-fighting, tight-knit squad here. We don't put up with a lot of shit. We're out to kill fucking gooks and always wanna be the first in and best at the toughest jobs. I, uh, wanna walk point-squad on sweeps. We want the hardest patrols. We are the very fucking best in all Charlie Company. For sure."

This was coming straight out of the mouth of the guy who is my direct superior. He's a sergeant; I'm a hapless private. And he has a macho desire to get into the shit that is going to get me killed.

Stotka continued, "Of course, Hoss, you gotta realize that you aren't gonna be carrying that twinky little M-79 for long."

I thought of my sweet grenade launcher back at the hooch. I'd grown rather fond of "Little Mike." It felt as comfortable in my hands as my well-used pocketknife.

"You're a big guy, you should be humpin' the 60. We'll try and get you into that job. Of course, the lifespan of an M-60 gunner can be shorter than just about anybody's but the lieutenants and me out here."

Then Stotka launched into the whole gung-ho soldier routine again. I was dazzled. Worried, but dazzled.

Boise Buddies

Chapter 2: Mocking fate

The current that swept me into Firebase 30 was flowing past me 16 months before, in August of 1967, the summer after high school graduation. In the dry August heat of Boise—a Western backwater where times could've easily passed for a decade earlier—my buddies Roger Jahnke, Richard Mattson and I hopped into my mom's '58 Bel-Air and headed for the Navy recruiting office.

Our decision to "by God, go down and enlist" was, in the finest tradition of aimless almost-men, totally ungrounded in common sense.

Mattson's dad had died a few months before, and his loss seemed to magnify our unmade career choices and uneventful days. Jahnke and I weren't fighting any particular devils, just ready to move on.

So we parked on Main Street, marched past the posters bright with crisp young sailors and found ourselves in front of the recruiter. He looked up.

"Yes?"

"We want to enlist in the Navy," one of us croaked.

The recruiter's eyes brightened. He straightened his back, leaned forward in his chair and motioned for us to sit.

"Very good. Here's some brochures to show you what today's Navy has to offer," he said, pulling pamphlets, forms and pencils from his desk drawer. "What are you guys interested in? Of course, you can get any job that you want in the Navy. Unlike the Army or the Marine Corps, we stress things you like to do, that you want to do."

He turned to Roger. "What are you looking for? What do you want in a career?"

"I'm into free-form music. I want to be a musician, a composer," Jahnke replied. "I don't want to be just a band musician."

"Well, all we've got in the Navy is bands," the recruiter said. He turned, his voice raised hopefully, to Mattson.

"And what do you want to be?"

"Well, I like to write," said Mattson, launching into what Jahnke and I had come to recognize as his post-high-school diatribe. "I want to be a writer. A novelist, maybe."

"We obviously don't have anything like that. Maybe you could be a clerk typist." The recruiter shoved an appropriate form at Mattson and turned, with something less than enthusiasm, in my direction.

"And ... you?"

"Well, all I know how to do is be an artist. I was hoping maybe you guys would have something along the lines of, you know, illustrating or making charts and graphs."

The recruiter sank back in his swivel chair, which was chalky government green.

"Of course, you three realize that jobs like you asked for are hard to come by. People get them in the service and stay in them for years and years. They just don't come up. Is there anything else you would take?"

We allowed that we weren't really sure.

"Look, you take this stuff and you guys get out of here and leave me alone. You finish school." The recruiter stood up. "Maybe you can get into ROTC in college, I don't know. But don't come back here. It looks like you guys want to live a fairyland life and that's not what the Navy has to offer."

The recruiter's wiry neck and face had reddened above his starched collar. He showed us to the door.

We fumbled back onto Main Street and climbed into the turquoise Chevy, cursing the unreasonable nature of the asshole recruiter. After half an hour of cruising around town, we calmed down enough to consider our next step – that is, which recruiting office to try next.

I offered: "Well, I don't really want to go into the Air Force. My dad was in the Air Force."

Jahnke said: "And I really don't want to go into the Marine Corps—Jesus!"

Mattson and I chorused amen to that. "Jesus! I don't want to join the Marines."

So we marched over to the Army recruiter. It was the same story, only worse.

"We just don't have anything for you," said the rather forlorn, khaki-clad, colorfully badged and ribbon-bedecked sergeant. "We can't guarantee that you'll get what you want. Right now we need people in combat arms."

The next stop was Albertsons supermarket, where Jahnke, who looked the oldest, bought some Coors. We drove out to Robie Creek and spent the afternoon sitting around, drinking beer and talking about how miserable we were. Then we drove back into town.

At the end of the summer, Mattson and Jahnke headed off to college.

I spent that fall traveling, escaping with my folks' grudging permission to points east. Oklahoma, Louisiana, Florida, Michigan. I checked in with and mooched off relatives along the way, but otherwise was free to find myself. The search included a stint as a canal digger in Florida, where I discovered the joys of backbreaking labor and the charms of redneck kin but definitely did not discover myself.

Back in Idaho, the last of my Florida earnings having gone for plane fare, I was faced with the specter of the classroom. I went back to the Army recruiter.

From what the guy had told me previously, I understood that I'd get the job I asked for if I signed up for a combat arm. I considered my options: infantry, armor, artillery.

Well, shit, it certainly wouldn't be the infantry. In armor, I'd get to ride around in tanks and stuff. That wouldn't be too bad, but I wasn't sure if my innate clumsiness could be overlooked or trained out of me. Artillery sounded good. I could sit back some 15 miles and lob shells on bad people and drink beer all day, which, I concluded much later, was a good assessment.

"I'd like to get into a combat arm, sign up for armor or artillery, or maybe MPs," I hesitantly told the recruiter.

"I'm sorry, Mr. Myers, but we can't take you."

I gave an incredulous look.

"Because you wear glasses. We cannot accept anyone into a combat arm or into any physical, intense activity of this type who wears glasses. You'd lose your glasses or otherwise could experience sight problems."

The recruiter did seem somewhat sorry, if not for the red-haired kid in front of him, then at least for a recruitment quota that was short of being filled. He seemed to view the poor vision in question as something I was trying to foist on his country and its Army. That's something that he, as a recruiter, must guard against.

"You know, you have to work for the betterment of everybody, not just yourself, Mr. Myers."

By the same token, if I wanted to sign up for some non-combat job, I was more than welcome to do so. "But, of course, we can't guarantee you'll get the job you'll ask for." What a deal! So if I wanted to sign up for ice cream machine repairman or some other phony-ass job for three years, I'd be good enough for them. But they couldn't even guarantee I'd be working on ice cream machines. So what was the point? For the spring semester, I gave myself to Boise State College, which in return gave me a row of D grades. It wasn't a completely bad time. There were plenty of empty hours for bullshitting with fellow academic delinquents. And there was my job driving a delivery truck for Betty Feeney's Decorator Shop. No joy in itself, it did strengthen my friendship with my "boss" and former Borah High classmate, Dave Mueller.

But those Ds settled in on me like the winter fog that crept over the foothills and down into my backwater town. D for duly depressed, D for deadly dull, D for damned tired of a sepia-tinted monotonous life. School offered no escape. Even if I could stomach another semester, it was unlikely the college would take me back. The campus was as dismal as the river that ran past it—the cold river that might have offered escape to a depressed man without a spark of youth left in him. But an end in the river would have been lacking in purpose or adventure. If I had to be cursed by a dull life, I would at least mock fate by demanding an interesting death.

I decided to volunteer for the draft.

This was a quick splash. None of that floundering around in the recruiters' quagmire of brochures and B.S. Just a brief encounter with a brusque woman with a poufed-up hairdo. She was the sole clerk working through the lunch hour at the draft bureau.

When I ambled in, she looked up from her desk and pushed her heart-shaped glasses farther up her nose. I stated my mission.

She walked to a huge wall of filing cabinets, pulled open a drawer, took out a piece of paper, and said "sign here, here and here." I did. She took the paperwork back and said: "You'll be getting your notice in the mail, thank you very much."

She put the form in another folder in another filing cabinet and slammed the drawer shut.

I walked out thinking, hell, this is really no big deal.

I went home and plopped my butt down on my bed. Then I went into the kitchen and sat at the vinyl-topped table, and argued with my folks until they accepted the finality, if not the rationality, of what I'd done. I was surprised by the strength of their objections, given ours was a longtime Air Force family. I grew up around men in uniforms.

"Goddamnit, son," said my dad, a retired flight engineer who worked as a night shift guard at the state penitentiary. "What the hell did you up and do that for?"

Mom was flustered. She was a hard-working accountant, and I guess in her motherly way she didn't like how my future was adding up.

I drove the couple of blocks to tell my buddy Mueller, melodramatically, that I didn't expect to live past 25. I was truly excited at my new prospects.

The next afternoon, when I got home from Betty Feeney's, my draft notice was in the mailbox.

Basic

Chapter 3: A dubious honor

Figuring I had several weeks to laze about before I was fully in Uncle Sam's grasp, I was relatively calm the morning I reported to the windowless, cinderblock recruitment center for my pre-induction tests and physical. The June sunshine was just as bright when I walked back into it later that morning, but its warmth seemed to have waned … along with my calm.

I had been poked, prodded, pinched and peered into. My poor eyesight had been cursorily tested and shrugged at, my state of mind approved, my form-filling patience taxed. Then, with an oath administered by a bored-looking lieutenant, I was in the Army.

I was given three hours to get to the airport for the trip to Fort Lewis, Washington.

Within those few flustered hours, I got into the Chevy and drove quickly downtown to Betty Feeney's to bid adieu to Mueller. In my preoccupation, I didn't see the car ahead that was turning out of a bank parking lot. I ran into it. The other driver and I surveyed the vehicles and decided that any damage was strictly to our nerves.

I managed to see Mueller, pack a bag and say gut-wrenching goodbyes to my folks and my younger brother, Ken. By the time I returned to the recruitment center, I was frazzled enough to plop onto a seat in the Army van and let them drive me where they would.

I was one of eight recruits taken to the Boise airport. Our chauffeur handed us our tickets and used one of those everyday farewells that people don't even hear, usually, but that struck me as slightly strange. "We'll see you guys later." Yeah.

The snowcap on Mount Rainier, which I could see from the Friendly Skies, was icing on the cake of a beautiful Northwest day. There was a breeze as the plane landed at the Seattle-Tacoma airport. Even the jet-fuel-and-rubber smell of the runways was lost in the air, which smelled sweet, like it had been washed.

The stewardesses had unnaturally bright, but sincere, smiles. We recruits, in an anxiety-loves-company surge of lightheartedness, felt a kind of bravado. We pulled combs from our back pockets to primp and brushed up on our favorite dirty jokes.

Even the gruffness of the sergeant who was waiting at the bottom of the ramp didn't stifle our cockiness.

"All right, you people," the sergeant barked. "Fall in over here, stand shoulder to shoulder, gear in front of you. Form a second single line here, everyone facing forward."

About 40 guys shuffled into two lines facing the two chartered buses.

"Shut up, put out your cigarettes, give your gear to the driver, he'll stow it, then get on!"

The talk was still pretty big—"Shit man some groovy shit!" "Look at these sorry civilian assholes"—but the landscape began to dim as the buses traveled the stretch of interstate that bisects Fort Lewis. Everybody was decidedly quieter by the time we found ourselves inside the snot-gray base.

The reception center that was home for the next week was like a fortress within a fortress. It was a world composed largely of barracks and mess halls. The buildings were outlined by white rocks that seemed to be all that kept their gray walls from melting into the gritty, cigarette-ash, grassless ground.

Whoever said oil and water don't mix was unfamiliar with the Fort Lewis reception center. The king of this hill was the mess sergeant, and grease hung like incense over his domain. It blended with the dampness in the air. Not even the frequent midsummer drizzles could remove it.

This slick humidity hit my square jaw at 4 a.m. as I rose to my first reveille, my first day of Army life. What my barracks mates and I formed that morning could only loosely be called a formation. But if we did not know how to line up or stand up or measure up in any way, we would learn by the end of the week.

We learned how to dress, how to salute, how to police the barracks. We learned how to say "yes sir," "no sir" and who to say "yes sir, no sir" to. It was like going to grade school. A new trainee had a daily list of things and actions to memorize. Who do you salute? When do you salute him? What do a first sergeant's rank chevrons look like? How do you blouse your trousers? Why? It was like being in the Bad Ass Boy Scouts. Be Prepared. Remember your chain of command. "My duty is to my country, sir!"

Much of the responsibility for teaching these rudiments of military life fell to the training cadre. Besides impressing upon our young minds the ways and means of their particular military occupational specialties (MOS), cadre members offered us wide-eyed trainees a glimpse of our own futures if we survived to become cadre ourselves.

A cadre was a three-chevron, E-5 buck sergeant, usually an infantryman finishing his two-year hitch in the States after serving in combat. Instead of the Smokey Bear hat and chest insignia of the drill sergeant, he wore a glossy green helmet liner that was encircled by a white stripe and fronted with the gold training center insignia.

Our cadre sergeant was dark, tall, pencil-thin and almost pretty enough to be a lounge-lizard. If it hadn't been for his parade-ground bearing and the occasional bitterness that glazed his eyes, it would have been hard to believe he had been anything as tough as a foot soldier. He'd been back from Vietnam for two months. His name, to the snickering delight of all the underage whiskey connoisseurs under him, was Jim Beam.

Beam almost never smiled, but there were signs that he was warming up to the people around him. That first week, as the new platoon was settling in, he could lean against a bunk, start talking about the war and instantly attract a crowd. We hung on every word of Beam's stories: the nighttime mortar attacks, murderous firefights, hot LZs, debilitating heat and mountain cold. He was a good card player and broke the rules by taking some of the rowdier soldiers into the latrine to play poker. I figured he must be trying to buddy up to us. He was living the same miserable life we were, concerning himself with shining boots and yes-sirring and marching around in the cold at 04:30.

Up to this point, Vietnam was a kind of netherworld to us. We knew it existed, we knew we didn't want to go there, but nobody was absolutely sure why not. Beam brought our blurry fears into focus with his stories about the 4th Infantry.

"God," he said as he slapped down his cards on the latrine floor. "The Cav units get to ride around in helicopters over flat paddies and sit on their fat asses and drink beer and Cokes and screw mamma-sans. And the funny 'n' fightin' 4th has to pound up and down the mountainsides, dig holes and squat in the fuckin' jungle and get mortared and rocketed for weeks on end. Trust me, it's fuckin' terrible."

His poker partners and hangers-on shifted uncomfortably as Beam told about the nasty night his platoon got mortared. The guy in the foxhole next to his was hit with shrapnel or a sliver of wood.

"It stuck in his head, just above his temple. There was nothing we could do for him. We couldn't get any choppers in, it was nighttime, gooks were inside our perimeter and anybody crawling over to help him would get shot. We had a couple or more guys get wounded and one killed trying to get to him. So he screamed all night long. All fucking night long he screamed. I can still hear him screaming.

"We were on that operation for two more weeks with 14 more casualties. We rode out on trucks."

Someone exhaled cigarette smoke with a strange sigh. Others coughed. The only other sound was the bumping and popping of the plumbing.

It was Beam who maneuvered us through our first momentous day. After breakfast and roll call came haircuts: short sidewalls, sideburns and a tousled top. Then cadre Beam whipped his civvie-clad charges into the reasonable facsimile of a platoon formation and introduced us to Drill Sergeant Lehi, our lord and master for the next eight weeks.

Beam turned to Lehi and apologized for the sorry condition of this group of useless dickheads. Lehi struck me as a short, pissed-off, unpleasant little shit. I was correct. Under his charge, the level of loudness and abuse stepped up. Good ol' boy Jim Beam became Sgt. Beam, callous shithead and Lehi's little lickspittle. Lehi began inspecting his new charges, one by one, questioning people's sexual orientation or parentage, observing personal hygiene problems and dropping a select few for push-ups. All this at the top of his lungs. From this moment, every action we took, meal we consumed and bit of sleep we attempted was done at an accelerated pace. "What a goddamn, fairy-ass group of shit-wipes. You bunch of sorry wastes of time will get straightened around. Well ... won't you?"

"Yes, drill sergeant!"

Lehi continued the sweet talk as he accompanied the group on a cattle-car transport to a vast supply depot, where we got our clothing issue. Throughout the day, the drill sergeant got personal with his observations and proclamations, looking an offending trainee in the eye and yelling, "You dipshit, you lil' puke. Drop 'n' gimme 15.

I don't even wanna look at your fucking face anymore." Then he'd boot the sweating push-upper from behind.

We formed up at supply for a cafeteria-style dispensing of our olive green underwear, socks, boots, fatigue pants and the rest of our everyday gear. The little Jewish-looking fellow who measured us must have misread his tape, because I somehow ended up with shirts and coats that were outsized even for my 250-pound frame.

Next, we trooped into a classroom and were lectured by MPs on the severity of punishment to be meted out to any of us found in possession of contraband items. One last chance was being given to divest ourselves of the nasty, naughty stuff.

Chosen as always for my presumably intimidating size, I was told to pass a box, like an usher in church, up and down the rows. When I was finished, the box was filled with knives, guns, girly magazines, even a pair of brass knuckles. As promised, people were frisked on their way out for any personal items not on the Army's approved list. We all made it into formation, and marched off hefting our full barracks bags. We marched the mile and a half back, in the rain. No buses this time.

Are you tough?

Back in the barracks, we had a few hours to write letters, shine shoes and pack up our civilian belongings for shipment home. Into my box went my brown and blue striped shirt, green Levis, white socks, black wingtips. Onto my back went the green fatigues. I pulled on the miraculously well-fitting black boots and stepped from the ranks of teenagers to the ranks of soldiers.

My public transformation into a raw private in no way ended the turmoil that I felt. I had traded aimlessness—and freedom—for a rather desperate shot at adventure. I'd handled guns since I was a kid. But was I a marksman? Could I make my god-awful out-of-shape body handle an obstacle course? Would I become a man? Could I, if it came to that, kill a man? I bit my nails, clenched my teeth and prayed to whomever that I could make the grade. I didn't have to be the best. Stooping over my footlocker that was like every other one, putting away gear that was like everyone else's, I just wanted to fade into this great, green group of men and survive.

The barracks were quiet. We weren't allowed to talk. But suddenly, I felt that I was the center of attention. I spun around to find Lehi looking me up and down.

My heart went into my throat and I started to sweat.

"Private, I want to see you in the unlocked room upstairs. Now."

What have I fucking done? What did I fucking do? Wait a minute. I hadn't had a chance to do anything wrong yet. As Lehi turned on his heels and walked over to size up someone else, I laid down the pairs of socks I'd been arranging and double-timed it up the stairs.

There was nothing in the room but an unused bunk. Lehi arrived and closed the door behind himself.

"What's your name, soldier?"

"Grady Myers, sir."

Lehi looked at the roster in his hand and whistled when he saw my age.

"Are you tough, Myers? Can you fight?"

"Yes sir, I suppose so—"

"Are you mean?"

"Only if I'm personally provoked, sir."

"Do you think you could whip me?"

"No, sir."

"Can you give men orders without asking them?"

"I don't know, sir. I've never tried."

"Well, you'll get a chance to try now. I'm making you platoon guide. I expect you to oversee these dickheads downstairs. You'll see that they do what they're told when they're told. I don't expect any failures. You're big enough to handle them. You'll get some help from me, but you'll be ultimately responsible. Do you understand?"

"I guess so, sir."

"What if I give you an order to give an order and someone refuses to carry it out? What are you going to do?"

"Well, sir, if they refused, and you weren't around..."

"And I wasn't around."

"I guess I'd use physical force if I had to, sir."

"That's what I wanted to hear, Myers. Remember, something goes wrong, it's on your back. Any questions?"

Damn right. Like: Why me? Here I wanted to melt away into this Army and you put me right on the firing line. Don't you know this is the last thing I want? What am I supposed to do, say "no thanks"? Why did you give me a job I can't possibly hope to fulfill?

"No, sir, no questions."

As soon as I was dismissed, I remembered what Lehi had said to the company earlier in the day: "Don't call me 'sir.' I'm not a sir, I work for a living!"

Half an hour later, I got a dark blue felt armband that had a buck sergeant's stripe sewn on it. The non-adjustable band was missing one of its three snaps and wouldn't reach around my large sleeve, so I fastened it with safety pins. I was the proud wearer of a phony sergeant's stripe hooked on with safety pins.

The stripes were given to me at evening formation. Also singled out for the dubious honor was fellow Boisean Gary Betchan, who was named platoon leader (another ersatz sergeant) and two guys who were designated squad leaders (phony corporals). Lehi ordered us to stand in front of the formation. He tapped us on our shoulders, one at a time, and told the others that they were to take orders from us or there would be hell to pay. I couldn't look at the men still in line.

So each morning at 4, I found myself barking orders at 40-some men to get out of bed and fall into line. I was the one who made sure housekeeping chores were done, who supervised issuing of gear, who served as an anchor in formation for others to fall in around.

I was reasonable about relaying orders and succeeded in talking down those few shitheads who balked at them. But unlike Betchan, a three-year enlistee who seemed to relish his authoritarian role (and was derisively called a goddamn lifer by the others, all draftees), I never felt comfortable mouthing orders. The role of taskmaster fit me like the oversized raincoat I was issued.-

Sometimes I got to thinking there really was something to this platoon guide business. On our last day at the reception center, a real soldier drove up to deliver the white unit-designation tapes that would identify the men when the platoon moved on to basic training. He came in the back door of the barracks and looked up at me as I was heading down the stairs. "Well, sergeant, where do I put these things?" he asked.

But I didn't feel capable of leadership. Not like a real sergeant, who had the power to kick butt all over the room if he so desired. Not like the straight-backed cadre.

Those combat-hardened cadre characters were admired by all of us trainees. We also had another hero there, a rebel who sat butt-naked on an upstairs bunk of another barracks, staring out a window.

The sergeants and their ilk were told not to move him, and they couldn't get him to talk. He shit on himself, he peed on himself. He was like a vegetable with a butch haircut. When the men in my platoon noticed this guy, he'd been at his stunt for three or four days. He was at it for a full week before an ambulance took him away.

We thought, "Man, what a groovy-ass scam to get out of this hole." Everybody knew the guy was phony. At least, we thought we knew. Sure, it would be great to have balls and be like the cadre. But wouldn't it also be great to have balls and do something that fucking crazy? Lehi, who had disappeared after assigning the platoon leadership, was back on the scene at the end of our first week to march us to our basic training enclave, our new little world. He told us we marched like a bunch of old ladies with crabs.

The reception center process of erasing individuality was followed by the process of wiping out independence. MPs could haul in a trainee if he was doing what he shouldn't be. That is, if he was caught going to the PX, drinking soda or beer, watching or talking to girls, being seen anywhere off limits, or exercising bathroom privileges without direct permission. I theorized that, before long, I'd need permission to exhale and would get thrown in stir for five days on a charge of breathing out of sequence.

The only trainee in my platoon to consistently evade the MPs was a teenager of Asian descent with the unexpected name of Michael Dougherty. Mike's tactics were straightforward. If he wanted to go to the off-limits PX for some forbidden candy bars, he simply removed the white company identification patch from his shirt and walked in. Needless to say, he was popular. We'd learned the hard way that there was no legitimate procedure for getting snacks on base. On our first authorized trip to the PX, when we bought our authorized toiletries, we loaded up on everything from Milky Ways to Playboys—only to have our booty confiscated by the drill sergeant as soon as we hit the barracks.

Each training company had to have a carnivore nickname. My company, A Company, 4th Battalion, 2nd Brigade, was the Tigers. When the sergeant heard that I could draw, he had me paint tigers on four of the white rocks that fourth platoon trainees had to painstakingly arrange in front of our barracks.

Every time the men of A-4-2 went into a meeting hall, we would be reminded of our nickname. The officer or non-commissioned officer in charge would yell "Reddip—seats!" and everyone would sit down. "You people didn't do it fast enough! On your feet! ... Reddip—seats!"

We'd try it all again, in unison. Everything had to be in unison. "I want to hear nothing but the smacking of assholes on those chairs at the same time, people! Do it again! Reddip—seats!"

When we hit our seats, we had to croak "A-4-2, every man's a tiger, roar!" Every goddamn time. We thought, what a waste of breath. But then the company across from us had to squeak out "B-4-2, every man's a bobcat, growl!"

It got worse. I wondered when we would get to the dogs and the cats and the canaries.

The question of eating was much less a laughing matter. Meals were something the Army seemed to tolerate only as a means of generating KP duty. If they wanted us to eat, why would they give us three minutes in the chow line, three minutes at the table? Why would they let a sergeant tap a starving soldier on the shoulder and say, "You're finished, outside," way before his three minutes of scarfing down his bread and beans were up, and make him settle for what little food he could stuff into his mouth on his way to dump his unfinished chow in the trash?

Indigestion was standard operating procedure for our stomachs. Our minds weren't much better off, being so rarely nourished by more than five hours' sleep or 20-minute catnaps on cattle car trips to some training site. In order to get extra sleep, we'd keep our field jackets on and flop gently onto our tightly made bunks at night. If we didn't mess up the bedding, we didn't have to waste time in the morning getting the blankets smoothed flat as a board.

But sleep wasn't near the problem that hunger became. It seems as if the whole time we were mastering the art of the salute, learning what to, when to and how to polish, delving into the mysteries of our chain-of-command and practicing the myriad mechanisms of marching in formation, we were thinking about food.

For at least one guy, the tiredness and hunger were too much to bear.

It happened on a Saturday night, when we were looking forward to the one day of the week when we could write letters, smoke, listen to the radio and read. We'd just had our evening meal of hamburger surprise, beans and chocolate cake when a commotion arose on the formation area between the company's four barracks.

I walked to the window and saw the only other guy in my platoon as big as me. He had seemed a bit slow, mentally, but right now he was fast on his feet, running like hell. He had a cake pan under one arm and was being followed by two military police who had their hands on their guns and were blowing their whistles. One of the drill sergeants and some other people joined in, chasing the soldier in circles, cops-and-robbers-style. He twisted out of their grasp at each lunge.

Guys were leaning out of their windows, cheering him on to the disgust of the pursuers. Suddenly, the cake pan man was cornered. There was nowhere for him to go but up the outside stairs to the second floor wooden landing of fourth platoon's barracks. He started up the fire ladder to the roof but jumped back and bashed through the door, bowling over a few bystanders. He tossed the precious pan under a bunk as the MPs burst into the room. He kicked, he cried, he screamed. It took four men to hold him down.

Within five minutes, the whole company heard the story about how a cook had caught Ernie, who'd been on KP, stealing an "abandoned" chocolate cake off a table reserved for edible garbage.

Several soldiers retrieved the cake and were enjoying the extra dessert as the MPs shoved Ernie into a car. It was the last time anybody in the company saw him.

Grand-scale insanity

The problem with men who stole cake and sat in the nude was not that their actions were crazy, but that they acted alone. The Army thrived on craziness. But it had to be carried out on a grand scale.

A potent symbol of this was the floor in the center of our barracks.

"This is my personal floor," Lehi bellowed. "Don't ever put your filthy, fucking boots or feet on my favorite floor without my telling you to. You people don't walk here, you don't work here except to keep it polished. When you're stepping on this"—he strutted up and down the shiny linoleum—"you're stepping on part of me, and I will then stomp all over you. Am I clear?"

"Yes, drill sergeant!" we replied as a chorus. We were standing on the walkways to either side, near our bunks and lockers.

Halfway up the support beams flanking the floor were water- and sand-filled one-gallon coffee cans painted red and lettered with the word "butts." Just as the floor was not for walking on, it was verboten to put cigarette butts in the butt cans. Every day, the water in the cans had to be changed. Woe betide the sorry platoon whose butt-can water was not fresh.

Nothing, however, incurred the wrath of the drill sergeant like a marred or dusty or simply trod-upon floor. The punishment for any of these travesties was likely to be a miserable evening of low-crawling under the barracks or running around them with foot lockers held high. So the sergeant's fetish became the trainees' obsession. We got on our knees and rubbed Carnauba wax into the tiles, then used an electric buffer to work the paste into a perfect, high gloss, checkerboard pattern. Then we would find the agile 17-year-olds among us and throw them into the rafters to dust. You never knew when the drill sergeant might look up.

Lehi was no worse than any other drill sergeant when it came to enforcing the chicken-shit rules. In other matters, he was better than many. The rules may have been unfair, but Lehi wasn't. He was a professional who only once, in my experience, broke the rule against the use of violence on trainees.

I was outside our barracks with the rest of my platoon, cleaning weapons, following our sixth day on the rifle range, when two knuckleheads near me got into an argument, and started shoving and pummeling each other. Disregarding my shouts to "knock it off, slow down, cool it," the more hot-headed of the two pulled a forbidden live round from his pocket, chambered it in his M-14 and stuck the rifle in the other guy's chest. I leaned over and grabbed the rifle barrel, turning it up and away. The hothead started screaming at me and the other guy, snatched up his M-14 and was going to bash in his companion's head. From out of thin air, a drill sergeant from a sister platoon appeared, cuffed the hothead behind the neck and said, "I want you three to come with me."

He dragged the offender to the front of the command hut, where Lehi was doing paperwork in the orderly room.

"Yo, Drill Sergeant Lehi, I need you to step out here for a minute," the other sergeant said. "I just caught this sorry son of a bitch looking to shoot this here other private with a live fucking round."

Lehi took the M-14, looked in the chamber, shucked the offending 7.62 mm round into his hand and put it in his starched pocket. Then he grabbed the forestock and receiver of the rifle, instantly swinging the buttstock up into the offender's face, knocking out two teeth and getting blood all over the place. When the private fell whimpering to the ground, Lehi booted him back on his feet, jamming the muzzle into the kid's face.

"You wanna play sissy-ass games, you wanna fucking play sissy-ass games?" Lehi asked through clenched teeth. He was red in the face, barely in control.

"Calm down, buddy," said the other sergeant, grabbing Lehi's arm. He called the MPs, who took away the bloodied soldier and jailed him on the court martial offense of unauthorized possession of live ammunition and felony assault. The second man got a boot in the ass from Lehi, extra duty as punishment and an Article 15 reprimand on his record.

I'd done my best to fade into the background through all of this. But when he was done with the major players, Lehi turned to me.

"Can't you keep track of your fucking people? You're on my permanent shit list for this. Myers, I'm going climb all over your back and be twisting my boot up your goddamned ass every time I see you. Right now drag your sorry butt back to your platoon."

I dragged it back.

A dud, a nemesis

Darrel was a long-faced fellow from Idaho who could not hack the physical training. He failed most of the physical and mental tests, then failed the proficiency tests given so he could make up for the failures. The drill sergeant pushed him to a point that was painful to watch. Because the sins of one trainee—from inability to insubordination—were visited on the whole platoon, the other men joined in the sergeant's berating of the man they called Darrel the Dud.

Apparently, the Boise draft board was to blame for Darrel's sorry status. In the same overzealousness with which they'd ignored my bad eyes, they ignored Darrel's considerably more serious handicap. As I heard the story, Darrel had been in a severe accident as a kid and was left with a metal plate in his skull and metal hip joints. The Army apparently wouldn't let Darrel out on medical grounds and wouldn't let up on the pressure they put on him. So he split.

An AWOL soldier was a blemish on the captain's, lieutenant's and drill sergeant's crank-'em-out records, and the official wrath was vented on the missing man's platoon, especially on the platoon guide.

We trainees didn't know Darrel was planning to go AWOL. We didn't help him run off. But, because we didn't stop him, we had to do more exercises and listen to profane lectures on the subject of being absent without leave.

When Darrel disappeared, about the third week of basic, my own physical problems were becoming obvious. I could run the required eight-minute mile and get through the belly-scraping low crawl exercises to the drill sergeant's satisfaction. But, despite my otherwise strong muscles, my wrists and ankles were weak. Sometimes I fell down on the frantic sprints between net climbing and tunnel crawling on the obstacle course.

My real nemesis was the fucking playground-like horizontal ladders. They were everywhere on our part of Fort Lewis. We had to grab them, pull ourselves off the ground, and swing from bar to bar, hand-over-hand, down the line of 20 or so bars before turning around and repeating the exercise. Despite my constant attempts—the bastards even had us swing under a line of ladders before entering the mess hall—I couldn't propel myself along them for any length of time.

About five weeks into training, we were put through the first of two tests on the obstacle course. I was one of the last to finish. My failure was compounded by the razzing I got. Wasn't it funny that the big-guy phony sergeant couldn't hack it? I was quiet on the way back from the obstacle course. I showered, changed and went down to the orderly room.

"Private Myers requests permission to enter, drill sergeant."

"Permission granted," replied Lehi.

Then, as if I were talking to a high school counselor, I explained that I felt I should resign as platoon guide. Considering my dismal displays of physical ability, I didn't see how I could maintain any respect as the platoon guide. Lehi didn't look a bit surprised.

"All right, Myers. I'm disappointed, I expected more out of you. You had better get your damn shit together fast. Devote more time to this physical business. I'm going to be on your ass to pass that test next week. If you don't, we're going to have to recycle you and anyone else who doesn't live up to company standards. Now get out of here."

I was relieved and left with my pride somewhat intact. At least along with the shame, I'd had the sense of honor to quit, I thought as I went to tell my buddy Betchan—who, along with the original squad leaders, had long since been fired from his post as platoon leader. My phony chevrons went to some guy who immediately told me how he was going to get even for the orders I'd given in the past. But that was the least of my concerns because, true to his word, Lehi was on my ass.

Two days after I resigned, Lehi took me out to see just how hard I was trying to master the monkey-bar exercise. I set to it over and over, grabbing the bars and then sliding off after a few swings until skin ripped off my hands and I left blood on the metal. Lehi said I would have to make up some extra points on the obstacle course, because I obviously wasn't going to make any on this test.

"All you've proved to me is that you can tear up your fucking hands. Get over to the dispensary and get them wrapped."

I started to withdraw, talking less to my buddies as I became convinced that I wouldn't make it through the second test on the obstacle course. Which I didn't.

I was sent to a special training battalion to do nothing but intense physical training until I could pass the test.

That meant extending my basic training for four weeks.

I had spent the last few crowded weeks running and marching, rough riding in buses and cattle cars and hustling through hand-to-hand combat and bayonet classes. I threw grenades, breathed in riot gas, shot round after round on the rifle range, low crawled under barbed wire and sat through dozens of mostly forgettable classes. The whole time my stomach cramping and aching with anxiety and the fear of failure. I saw no relief.

Lockers Below

Chapter 4: The worst that ever happened

Shortly after I was told I'd be recycled, I was assigned to wash the second-floor barracks windows. A fellow trainee named Miller sat on the ledge of an open window, torso outdoors and legs inside. My job was to dip the rag in a bucket, wipe the inside of the glass, rinse the rag and hand it to Miller, who washed the outside before handing it back. This went on in a pleasant mindless way until, on the eighth window, I reached under the open sash to hand Miller the sopping-wet rag—and Miller wasn't there.

I looked out and down. Miller lay on the ground, out cold. I shouted to no one in particular: "Hey, Miller just fell out the window!"

Miller's back injury was minor, but enough to keep him in the infirmary for a few days. They decided to put him through the next training cycle. He and I waited together for the handful of days before our next cycle started and we could move on—me to the special training battalion, Miller into a new basic training unit.

While we waited, we remained in the fourth platoon barracks but were no longer assigned to them. We were given odd jobs. We spent the first day painting the kitchen in the cook hut. We were tired by the time we returned to the barracks about 19:00, and were lounging on our bunks reading the Sunday comics, which we'd scrounged from the cook, when we heard the drill sergeant's whistle. Miller and I were pleased that, for once, we could sit and ignore the shrill sound. We didn't have to fall out in formation.

A string of profanities floated up from the parade ground, but I couldn't make out what Lehi was yelling about. Suddenly, the whole building was rumbling with the sound of 80 booted feet running and 40 loud voices muttering. The trainees were frantically scurrying around, grabbing their footlockers. When Miller and I asked what going on, all we got in reply was, "You dopey fuckers, get outta the way... you ain't asked to do this shit."

Lehi's voice rose up the stairs. "You better fucking move... out here now!" as the men fell out with their footlockers.

Miller and I sneaked over to the window to watch. We didn't want to risk Lehi seeing us and demanding that we join the fun.

The drill sergeant had the men fall in line with their lockers held over their heads.

"You useless shits are too fucking slow! Do it again! Now!"

They ran crashing back into the building, then fell out again, their rattling footlockers held aloft.

"You lazy-ass people'r still too girly slow. Again!"

They painfully hustled back in. By then, everybody was wheezing and coughing under the weight of their 50-pound loads. They turned and fell back out. "'Bout goddamn time." Lehi said. "Now keep 'em up. H'right hace, double....time ... hr'uaahp." The trainees ran around and around and around the company quadrangle trying to keep the footlockers over their heads. Miller and I could hear the klunka! klunka! klunka! of the lockers' contents bouncing around.

After 10 minutes, Lehi broke up the parade and ordered them to put the footlockers away. The exhausted trainees ran back outside and fell into line.

"Now you've got five minutes to straighten out those footlockers. They're a goddamn mess. I want them cleaned up good or you fuckin' people will be low-crawling out here for five hours!"

They ran back in and started putting their socks and shaving kits back in order. I could hear Lehi storm in the door downstairs, march up and down "his floor" and roar, "By God, that ain't good enough!" and blow the whistle again.

The men were told to get into their wet-weather gear. They had to wear their rubber rain outfits while they low-crawled three times under the company's four barracks. Then it was back to straighten the footlockers. When Lehi came around to inspect, Miller and I fell into line. No one told us what had aggravated the drill sergeant.

The next evening was considerably quieter. The Tigers had gone on overnight maneuvers, during which they set up tents in the middle of the night so that the sergeant could kick them down.

After a rare long night's sleep, Miller and I roused ourselves. On his way to shave, Miller noticed the padlocks on the doors to the rooms where the phony sergeants slept had been cut. Inside, the lockers in which many of the trainees' radios and other valuables were kept had been broken into. He and I jogged to the duty hut and banged on the door of the orderly room.

"Permission to enter?"

"Permission to enter granted," replied the sergeant inside.

"Somebody broke into our barracks and stole a bunch of stuff out of the lockers!" I reported.

"You're shittin' me!"

"No, it's true," said Miller.

The three of us marched back to the barracks to survey the damage.

While Miller and I went off to do our painting for the day, the other barracks in the company were searched. Three of the four had been robbed.

Because Miller and I were the only soldiers who'd slept in the compound that night, we became suspects. The next day, we were questioned individually by agents from the Army's Criminal Investigation Division. For three hours, I sat at a desk and was grilled by two C.I.D. guys, one in a gray suit and one in a brown suit. When had I gone to bed that night? When had I noticed the thefts? Did I expect them to believe I'd actually slept through the sounds of hacksaws and clippers crunching metal 40 feet from my bunk? Although the C.I.D. couldn't find any evidence that we were involved in the crimes, I was left feeling the whole incident was another blotch on my record.

I felt uneasy for a week, until I heard that one of the training cadres and another guy had been arrested for the thefts, probably after they'd been caught trying to pawn the goods

To the breaking point

News about the arrests brought the only glimmer of relief to my life the following week because by then I was in the special training battalion.

The Special Training Company, 2nd Brigade, was the worst thing that had ever happened to me. The Army sent men there who weren't fit for immediate acceptance into active military service, who hadn't been able to make it through basic. For most of us, the problems were physical. Others simply couldn't speak English.

But the Army treated us all as mentally incompetent, as if we were all at the level of the slowest mouth-breathers among us.

When we fell into formation each day, we were checked to make sure we were properly washed, that our fingernails were clean. We were treated like inmates in an asylum, nothing but a bunch of duds.

We "special" trainees were up at 04:00 every day to begin 12 to 14 hours of physical training. Push-ups, sit-ups, pull-ups, running, low crawling. They gave me tennis balls to squeeze in hopes of strengthening my wrists.

We were given daily physical tests with the score tallied at the end of each week. The soldiers who did well in five tests would be sent back to regular basic training.

Adding to the degradation was the confusion caused by what was, from the Army's point of view, one of the great tragedies of my military career. I lost my goddamn dogtags.

It happened when I was low-crawling through a sand pit. I reported the missing tags, expecting to be told, "Oh, OK, we'll get you another set." But, no. The drill sergeant was at a loss about how to get them replaced. First, the sergeant had to find my files, and my files were not readily located. For days, while the search continued, I was less than persona non grata. I was persona nonentity. Take away a soldier's dogtags, and what is he? To add insult to injury, Idaho National Guard units were in camp at Fort Lewis when I was in special training. One of the units was assigned to my training battalion.

Of course, the Idahoans looked down the roster and saw I was the only one from the state among the duds.

"We don't want you in here screwing up the good name of our state," the Guardsmen would say. "So if you don't pass through this shit in a week, you'll find yourself dealing with the world-of-hurt we'll bring down on you."

I just wanted to be left alone.

I was tired of being labeled a fuck-up, of being identified with dullards. If I couldn't get out by passing those damn tests, I resolved to go AWOL. Another, not-so-dull soldier and I planned how we'd get out, without pausing to consider how we'd get our doughy special trainee bodies over 12 feet of chain link and barbed wire in the darkness. We would stay with the other guy's sister up in Bremerton and head to Canada from there.

Considering my emotions, going AWOL was a sane idea. The constant exertion, the abysmally low self-esteem, even the minuscule meals on the special trainees' diet—they were all driving me mad. I was told about a dud who had slashed his wrists the week before, only to be patched up and sent back. I was convinced that if I tried to off myself, I'd leave behind more than bloodstains on the latrine wall. I'd leave my life and everything behind, for good.

I was near the breaking point the Friday I had to take the tests. I still couldn't handle the goddamn horizontal bars, so I pushed myself on everything else. I passed by one point.

When it was over, a major from the Idaho Guard asked me how I'd done. When I said I'd passed, he slapped me on the back. "Outstanding," he said. "Glad to hear it!"

He wasn't one-tenth as glad as I was. On the ride back to the barracks, I sat by myself toward the front of the bus, choking back tears. The other guys, those who hadn't passed, didn't get near me. My buddy of the AWOL escape plan didn't even look at me. But he had finally passed, too.

I got my new orders. I was told to put myself and my stuff in a car, and was driven to another basic training outfit, E-3-1, a mile away. It wasn't going to be easy getting accepted by a bunch of guys who have been training together for more than five weeks. The camaraderie that I sometimes felt in my first outfit, A-4-2, was missing from this new one.

I was four weeks further along in training than these newer guys, even with my sorry "special training" side-trip. Another thing that set me apart was my expert marksman badge.

When I arrived, the company was going through its qualification range tests with the M-14 rifle, which I'd completed. The silver-oxidized medal pinned over my pocket meant I'd shot better than a sharpshooter (which meant a soldier was sharp enough to aim in the direction of the target and shoot) and much better than a marksman (someone who could aim, shoot and sometimes hit the mark). Only three of us in my original company had qualified expert, and I wasn't gonna put up with crap from any badgeless clowns in my new platoon when I wore my uniform to church that first Sunday. (Given the choice between church and KP, I was inclined to be religious. Besides, it was worth listening to a chaplain ramble on about God and guts when, after the service, we got to gorge ourselves on punch and cookies.)

For the first few days, while the others were on the rifle range, I pulled KP. I was emptying trash one afternoon when I looked up to see a military police car drive in with two MPs in front and Darrel in back. Darrel the Dud! They'd caught him after he'd gone AWOL and had returned his unfortunate ass back to Fort Lewis, this time to my new training company.

When Darrel was settled in to his platoon, I found him and asked, "What happened? How's it going?" only to get a mumbled, "I don't want to talk about it."

My questions may have been the most civil words uttered to Darrel since his return. He was just a "fuckin' puke AWOL sonofabitch" to many of the other trainees. They, along with the drill sergeants, wasted no opportunity to mock him. They told

Darrel that he'd better straighten up, because everyone knew that if he split again they would all be punished for it. He did, one week later, and they were. The punishment was under-barracks low-crawling, lots of it.

I never heard if the Army caught up with Darrel a second time.

I fell back into the training routine. Days were filled with classroom and physical training sessions. The only significantly different lesson took place during the night infiltration course.

We got to the course a couple of hours after sunset. At one end of the field was an eight-foot deep, wood-lined trench; at the other end, wooden bunkers that housed two M-60 machine guns loaded with live ammo. In the middle was a maze of rocks, barbed wire and barrels crammed with explosives. The barrels were surrounded by wire mesh that was supposed to contain any shrapnel.

The exercise involved the entire company, an operation on a grander scale than any I'd seen yet at Fort Lewis. More than 100 men crammed into the trench.

We'd been told what to expect as we scrabbled like land crabs or scooted like rats through the maze to the other end of the course. The explosives would be detonated and the machine guns would be fired in bursts well over our heads. We were to obey any loud-speaker instructions and, most importantly, we were to stay down. The instructors delivered the warning more strongly than usual because a trainee had been killed an hour before. He panicked, stood up, was shot and bled to death.

A whistle blew. We went over the top and began crawling toward the bunkers. The only light was from the constant flow of red tracers whizzing over our heads and from the barrels that exploded frequently in smoky flashes. It was like a noisy scene from a World War I movie, with gruff sergeants' voices growling from nowhere. It didn't last long. We were soon forming up and heading for bleachers, where we would be lectured on the exercise.

As we did, we heard a single bang and a lot of commotion back at the range. Dust was still settling in the night air. It wasn't a planned detonation. After the exercise, a machine gunner had flipped open the breach cover of his M-60 and was pulling back on the cocking handle when the last round exploded in his face. An ambulance roared up to the bunker. The range instructors and cadre were slow getting to our debriefing. As the officers stood around in front of the bleachers, I could hear the tension in their voices. Two men had been lost in one night—one of them their friend. There would be questions to answer.

I continued to feel like a Johnny-come-lately in my platoon. Several days without a bunkmate added to the social isolation. On the third or fourth night, I grumpily woke up to the sound of someone fumbling in the other footlocker.

"Hey, what the hell are you doing? Moving in at night?" I asked the shadowy figure. He whispered, "I'll tell you about it in the morning."

By the morning light, the shadow turned out to be a nondescript little guy who wore thick eyeglasses. He had been the only black in his last platoon, which included three white hard-asses from the South who made no secret of their racism. They beat him severely, saying they were going to kill him next time. When they came after him again, he grabbed a pipe from some plumbing supplies in the barracks hallway and ran into a cadre room upstairs. The Southerners charged up the stairs after him, bragging that they were going to break his nigger neck. He hit two of them with the pipe, breaking one attacker's arm and giving a concussion to the other.

After that, he told me, he locked himself in the room for a day and a half until a black officer coaxed him out saying: "We're going to get you away from here. We know these guys are assholes. We'll make it safe."

They quietly moved him to E-3-1. He and I, both misfits of a sort, got along well. Once his story got around, none of the redneck rough types ever hassled him.

Drill sergeant blues

I rarely thought about race relations at Fort Lewis. The way I saw it, the Army shit on everybody fairly equally. And that shit could fall on you from a black source as easily as from a white one. My new drill sergeant was proof of that.

This guy may have been responsible for the tension and lack of morale in the platoon. Drill Sgt. Sherman was about 30, a two-tour Vietnam veteran who could be pleasant enough one moment and then be pissing on everyone's backs the next. Once, when we'd returned from a long day of training, Sherman decided the barracks weren't tidy enough, so he went through the usual routine of making people do PT and push-ups. He then gave us 15 minutes to police the place.

When he came to inspect our efforts, he opened the second footlocker and found a gum wrapper in the top tray among the neat array of shaving gear that was meant only for display. He started bellowing at the top of his lungs, turning cherry red around the edges of his chocolate face.

On his orders, everyone fell out into formation. It was pouring, and we weren't wearing rain gear. A terrible shattering racket came from our barracks. It frightened the living shit out of us. The sergeant was yelling, barking, snapping and howling. We couldn't understand a word. It got quiet for a minute, then he shouted for us to double-time our sorry asses back inside.

My God! The results of this one man's mayhem stunned us stupid.

He had picked up every footlocker and dumped the contents into a huge pile. He pulled down all the standing lockers. He tossed our uniforms in the middle of the highly polished drill sergeant's floor, then dumped and scattered boxes of our laundry powder and bleach over everything, then poured water from the butt cans on top of the mound, then kicked and stirred it all around with his boots. He broke light fixtures, tore racks off the walls and threw the butt cans around.

Then Sherman stood tall in front of the soggy platoon and said we had 35 minutes to clean up the mess.

It took us 30 minutes just to sort out our gear. What we managed to distinguish as our own was hardly worth salvaging. My uniform, like the layers of Carnauba wax on the drill sergeant's floor, had been ruined by the detergent. If I tried to wear it in its bleached-out condition, I would have been written up.

Of course, we weren't able to get the barracks in order within 35 minutes. As punishment, the sergeant made us low-crawl under the barracks, which meant when we returned we got mud on top of the rest of the mess.

The company commander was coming for an inspection the next day, so no one got any sleep. Because it was against the rules to be up after curfew for any reason, we posted guards outside, tacked blankets over every window to keep the lights from being seen, and spent the night trying to put things in order. We must have passed inspection but our savaged barracks never fully recovered.

Sherman also ruined my one night as a guard for the company area. It was pleasant duty. Two men patrolled, trading off every two hours with another duo assigned to the largely symbolic military routine. It was one of the few times the trainees had access to the dayroom, where the corporal of the guard had his desk and coffeepot. When he wasn't looking, we used what change we could scrounge to raid the candy machines. It was quiet, about midnight, when my companion challenged a tall figure staggering into the compound.

"Halt! Who goes there?"

"Who the fuck wants to know?" replied a belligerent voice that he knew only too well. The drill sergeant was in civilian getup and drunk.

"Just doing my job, sergeant," the slight soldier said.

The words were barely out of his mouth when the drill sergeant slammed a fist into his chest. I ran over to help as my fellow guard fell to the ground, his helmet liner skidding across the gravel.

I felt awkward. What in hell should I do, beat up my drill sergeant with my night stick? I helped the guard up and started fending off the inebriated sergeant. He spun around and ambled off into the darkness, muttering something unintelligible. The two of us reported the incident. There was nothing else we could do.

Our phony platoon leader made the perfect brown-nosing sidekick for Sherman, matching his sadistic side but never giving in, as the sergeant did in an occasional moment of decency.

The phony platoon leader had served a hitch in the Navy. Somewhere along the line, he'd decided that working as a supply puke on an aircraft carrier was not the kind of manly occupation for which he was so well suited, so he re-upped into the Army. He told everyone within hearing range that he was here to be a butt-kicking Ranger and Green Beret. "A fuckin' killer." He looked with open contempt on those who hoped they'd gather up jobs as cooks or mechanics.

"By God," he'd say. "I'm gonna be where the fuckin' fightin' is, not like you fucknuts. My mission's killing Cong."

With the drill sergeant's consent, this character did more than pass along orders. He gave them, and did so with apparent delight.

One of this guy's favorite targets was a reasonably nice, but not terribly astute, trainee whose most apparent fault was his aversion to showers. He stunk, and our phony platoon leader made a personal crusade out of straightening him out. The stinky troop was always the last out of bed and to fall into formation, making our phony leader look bad. One morning, the platoon leader told the others to stand to as he ordered this guy to get in and out, in and out, in and out of his top bunk. The Navy guy stood there yelling. "Get out, get out, get outta the bed—get up, get up, get up inn'a the bed." Up and down, in and out until the subject of the torment fell exhausted to the floor.

Another morning, the soldier had no intention of getting out of bed, having reported some illness and been given a "profile" note excusing him from the day's training. He was getting a whole training day in bed! Lucky bastard. When the platoon leader heard that, he and three of his henchmen—guys like that always had henchmen—dragged the soldier out of bed. They threw him into the showers, turned the cold water on and dumped laundry soap over him. They attacked him with floor brushes until his shorts and at least one layer of skin were scrubbed off. Then they chased him, naked, wet and sobbing, up to the second floor. They shoved and pummeled him back and forth, shouting threats. As a group of second-floor spectators gathered, the platoon leader pushed him halfway down the stairs. Raw and bloody nosed, he crawled back into his bunk. He was still lying there, quiet, under his Army blanket, when we returned to the barracks that evening. After that, the poor guy got quicker getting out of bed. And he took showers.

The appointed platoon guide was less sadistic but even more gung-ho than the platoon leader. He was a tall, blond kid whose father was an Army bird colonel from Fort Carson, Colo. His phony rank was a special source of pride for him, something to write home about. Two days before we finished basic, we marched through a graduation rehearsal. After the mock drills, we were in the barracks doing a final strip-down cleaning of our weapons. The platoon guide finished his M-14, then was called outside to break up a scuffle or some such. When he got back, his rifle was gone.

The Army had made it clear that a murder charge was comparable to—nay, preferable to—losing one's rifle. And for a phony sergeant to lose his rifle just before his military family was flying in to witness his graduation ... for him to lose his rifle was unthinkable.

The platoon guide was panic-stricken at the sight of the rifle rack, with that gaping slot in an otherwise orderly row of M-14s. He was sure, absolutely fucking positive, he had racked his rifle. He looked everywhere for the thing, with half the platoon joining in the search. When he felt the last possible hiding place had been ruled out, he lost control. He couldn't speak, he couldn't even control his bowels.

As other guys tried to restrain him, telling him to calm down, the drill sergeant stormed in. Someone had squealed.

The sergeant swore at, knocked down and kicked the platoon guide before ripping the buck sergeant brassard from his sleeve and throwing it at another trainee. When told to shut up and put the on the armband, the spanking-new platoon guide looked almost as scared and crestfallen as the old one.

The former phony sergeant was ordered to move out of the area reserved for the platoon guide. As he went, dejectedly, about the business of collecting his gear, he moved the bunk and saw his rifle stuck between the mattress and the wall. He sat down and sobbed. Those who had helped in the search adjourned to the latrine area in order to leave him alone. When they came out 10 minutes later, he'd snapped out of it. He didn't have any real buddies, anyway, but he also didn't seem to have any real enemies. We never learned who hid his rifle.

Sometime during the week before graduation, we were marched to a post theater-assembly hall to pick up our orders. From a row of tables set up in front of the auditorium, we picked up the brown envelopes that contained our fate. I opened the crisp white paper slowly to reveal my military occupational specialty (MOS). The verdict: 11Bravo20, light weapons infantry.

I would be a grunt. I told only my bunkmate and maybe a couple of other guys.

Some men were less hesitant to share their news. The phony platoon leader waved his orders under the noses of others, boasting that he was going into the infantry. So we were astonished when, on the morning of graduation, we heard the rumor that the tough-talking Navy guy had his orders changed. The standard reaction was "What th...? I've never seen anybody want to get into the infantry more than that stupid shit." It figured.

On the afternoon of that Friday, September 13, 1968, we fell in for our graduation parade-by and review. We wore our short-sleeved summer-tan, class B uniforms, complete with web gear, canteens, bayonets, rifles and helmet liners. Our trousers were bloused into our gleaming boots as we marched, shoulder arms, onto the parade field.

Four companies were graduating that day and the men in each passing platoon of each passing company turned their heads, saluting our nation's colors presented in front of a row of bleachers, where officers and civilian relatives were sitting. The soldiers were all trying to get a look at the legs of the women in the crowd.

My platoon took special notice of the bird colonel from Fort Carson. The former platoon guide's sister was there, too, decked out in a yellow dress and standing coyly next to her mother, who looked like she'd stepped off the set of "Leave It to Beaver."

After hearing a speech about how wonderful we were for fighting for the country, we marched back to our company area and formed up into our last E-3-1 platoon formation.

"All of you people who have infantry school orders will retain your web gear, your canteen cover and your bayonet scabbard. Your canteen, bayonet and rifle will be returned to the company armory," the company's first sergeant said. "All other personnel who are going into other MOSs will put their helmet liners in the helmet liner pile, their web gear in the web gear pile and their canteens in the canteen stuff piles and fall back to their respective platoons. Fall out!"

I checked in my bayonet and rifle and joined in the rush of men who were gladly packing to leave the barracks for good. The whistle trilled, we fell back into formation as fast as we could, dropping our duffel bags beside us and standing at attention. Drill sergeants walked up and down, looking at their charges, giving them hell, yet again, for being the worst outfit they'd ever seen.

I glanced around at the others in my platoon and noticed I was the only one wearing a helmet liner and sporting web gear. Everyone else was crowned with green, peaked garrison caps—aka, cunt-caps—and wore no web gear. I was the solitary Eleven Bravo Twenty.

Drill Sgt. Sherman stood back and scowled. "Lose those fuckin' smiles! You goofy shitbags. There's just one man with big, hairy balls among you bunch of dickless bastards. And that's Myers."

Despite myself, my chest swelled, a little. "He's going eleven-bravo, mutha'hump'n infantry. He's gonna be fuckin' dead a year from now, all worn out from greasing dinks so the rest of you slacking, sorry-assed, soft-dicked losers can sleep all safe and quiet-like! Now everybody drop and do ten for Myers."

I just stood there, stunned. Gazed down at them. Felt like a real soldier.

That little incident was forgotten as soon we broke ranks. The other guys were relieved they would end up as cooks and mechanics and tank drivers—or, in the case of the Navy guy, a supply clerk. They shook my hand, saying, "damn, man" or "too bad, man," or just waved their multicolored Northwest Airlines tickets at me as they snatched up their duffel bags and ran to the smoky, idling buses for Sea-Tac airport.

The gray-haired first sergeant came by to shake hands with me and a dozen or so other company grads headed for Advanced Infantry Training just a mile away, still on Fort Lewis. A small green bus, glinting in the orange late-afternoon light, came by and drove us across the large drill field to our new company areas.

We were infant infantrymen now.

Dickheads

Chapter 5: Changing fortunes

In basic training, we'd often stare at the burly AIT units double-timing breathlessly past us as we marched. Like everyone else, I knew those guys were headed for Nam. And, like everyone else, I'd heard that 80 percent of Fort Lewis Infantry School grads ended up wounded or KIA. I'd just nod while others talked shit about those "sorry, simple AIT bastards working so hard to get hurt" while they were looking forward to safe jobs baking bread, typing reports or repairing jeeps. I watched fascinated as those infantry trainees, M-16s slung tightly over their shoulders, ran by us in rhythmic cadence, bellowing lusty lyrics, their guidon bearer leading the way. While I was sliding toward zero self-esteem, they were confident, powerful and, well, heroic.

Initiation into AIT didn't begin immediately for me and the other trainees who gradually reported to the orderly room after graduation from basic. We didn't have to show up until reveille the next morning, but we didn't have passes to leave the base. I ended up at a crowded Enlisted Men's "Club" that served nothing but nasty 3.2 beer and Radarange sandwiches. I spent my few free hours watching the comings and goings of this human anthill.

At dawn, we fell into loose formation and met the men in charge of our company. Several drill, platoon, and helmeted cadre sergeants would supervise our AIT transformations. The drill sergeant I dealt with most often was known (behind his back) as WD, for Walkin' Dead. He weighed about 110 pounds, had a sallow complexion, 120 years of pimples on his 25-year-old face and a strange accent that no one could immediately place. It turned out that he was a "dishonored son" of a disinherited British lord. He had immigrated to the U.S. and joined the Army while retaining his British citizenship. He was an obnoxious, mean-spirited chap who approached life as if it were a bizarre joke.

Our platoon was led by two buck sergeants, recent "Shake 'n' Bake" graduates of the 21-week NCO school at Fort Benning, Ga. They had to serve a tour in charge of a training platoon before being sent overseas. One of them, the platoon leader, was a tall, puffy-faced Midwesterner who got along with everyone. The other, the platoon guide, was a scrawny ROTC alumnus who got along with no one.

The trainees figured it this way. The platoon guide had a bad case of the ass because everybody was down on him for having a harelip. Nobody was down on him for having a harelip. But he wanted everybody to be down on him because of his harelip, so he chewed everybody out because he had a harelip. Something like that.

The deformity became annoying not because of the way the man looked, but because of the way he sounded. He lisped, which in conversation was tolerable. But a man who lisps while he counts cadence is something else again. For several weeks we listened to "huff, toofth, hrff, horfth."

The lisping started out as a platoon joke. But pretty soon his "ifth-ing" grated on us. Then one day, when we were in a practice formation for a ceremony, the training brigade commander heard the lisp rasping across the parade ground and asked the platoon guide to knock off his cadence counting because it was an embarrassment.

Months later, I heard that our harelipped sergeant lasted about a month in Nam before being listed MIA.

I made some friends. One of them was Lowell Nutz, a former Iowa crop-dusting pilot whose name always elicited snickers despite his insistent reminders that it was pronounced "newts." Nutz was 27—ancient in the eyes of his teenage friends. We were always watching out for him, because we knew he needed a lot of rest after the rigors of training. When the platoon guide came around looking for someone to fill this or that detail, my buddies and I would steer Nutz to the back of the barracks and hide him under a mattress, where he could nap undisturbed. Then they would pull his KP duty for him. Nutz was, after all, 27 years old.

Another senior citizen in the AIT company was about 25. He was short and swarthy with a dark beard-shadow, square jaw and thick German accent. One day, MPs came and led him away. As we trainees heard the story, he was Ludwig Von Something-or-other and was AWOL from the Austrian army. He had come to America the year before and enlisted. No one knew why he escaped from one army just to join another.

My newest best buddy was Gary Lockhart, who bunked next to me. Lockhart was a blond, bright-eyed Minnesotan. Like me, he was a college dropout with similar ambivalent feelings about life in general and being in the Army in particular.

Lockhart and I were among the first in the company to make E-2. The elevation from E-1 meant that we'd been good soldiers, or something. I didn't know what I had done to deserve the stripe, but it evidently must'a been something wonderful. (Upon reaching Vietnam, one foot out of the plane's door, we automatically were promoted to E-3, Private First Class. Then the Army would have something to take from us if we lapsed into being bad soldiers.)

My fortunes changed in infantry training. For one thing, I didn't have to suffer through the indignity of failing the obstacle course again. Thanks to the company executive officer, I "happened" to pull KP and night guard both times the platoon went through it. Never in my life had I been so happy to empty trash and clean tables.

I was getting into fine physical fettle, but the painful memories of recycling didn't leave me. One day, 20 of us, out on some fool errand, watched a special training battalion work out. One of the trainees looked to weigh 300 pounds and stand 5-feet-5. He was in the low crawl pit not crawling low enough or fast enough. Two drill sergeants were shuffling in the dust alongside him, yelling at the guy as he rolled and flapped. My infantry classmates grimaced at the sad sight. "That poor fucker," someone said. "I can't believe that sorry shit, man. Nobody should be treated like that." I shook my head along with them, but the sad fact that I had been right there, doing that same thing a few weeks earlier, never came up.

As an infantry trainee, I faced an uncertain future. But the experience was pretty damned satisfying. Once at AIT, I cut off those over-pocket white tapes that marked me as a basic trainee. My scruffy olive drab helmet was handsomely covered with a reversible wide-leaf camo cover with a nifty, stretchy band. The old M-14, with its proud wooden butt stock, made way for the lighter plastic and aluminum M-16; when we marched, I held it tight against my back by its sling.

It wasn't necessary to see our different gear to identify us an AIT outfit. Even at a distance, you could spot us. We were the guys running. We ran everywhere. We rose an hour before reveille to run, then did calisthenics before running to breakfast. We ran to lunch and ran to dinner, and ran at double-time everywhere throughout the day.

All that running and PT'ing in the heat made for some sorry, gut sick, weak-legged infantry trainees. But when we found ourselves huffing past some pukes still in basic— or, best yet, some shapely femmes—we found that we could, indeed, take it some more. In a platoon-sized reflex action, we straightened our backs, held our rifles more tightly and bellowed our sing-song cadence even louder. We left open-mouthed admirers dazed and amazed in our dust.

It was the marching songs that kept infantry trainees from singing the blues.

Vulgar, nonsensical, tradition-bound, the songs provided the pulse that pushed blood through legs that should have stopped running, air through lungs that ached for rest.

At times the pulse was a simple "Airborne Ranger" chant, started by a leader and echoed by the troops.

"Sound off!" "One two!" "Sound off!" "Three four!" "Up th' hill, up th' hill ... "Down uh' hill, down uh' hill..." "All duh way, gotta go..." "Can't quit, won't quit... all uh' way ... "H'wan hwo'p, h'reep hor'p ... "

Sometimes it was a rhythmic shanty, like the one penned by our own company's exec: "We were down at the Ori-eh-en-tal, at the corner of the square-air-air, They were serving drinks as usual and the usual crowd was there-air-air. Let me go, let me go, Captain Li-it-tal and a good trainee I'll be-e-e, These infantry training blues are gonna be the death of me-e-e.

"On my right was private Rod-en-e-e-e, he was sliding from his chair-air-air, He was lying under the table and the usual crowd was there-air-air. Let me go, let me go, Captain Lit-it-al, and a good trainee I'll be-e-e, These infantry training bloo-uh-oos are gonna be the death of me-e-e.

"Upstairs was Sergeant Schwartzman's wife, her breasts were pink and bare-air-air. She was lying in bed as use-u-al and the usual crowd was there-air-air."

And there were the old classics: "I don't know but I've been told, Eskimo pussy's mighty cold.

"If I die in a combat zone, box me up and ship me home.

"If I die on the Russian front, bury me with a Russian cunt. Sound off!"

Sexual references were part of the training regimen from the first day of basic. More than once, we watched as a drill sergeant sent some idiot trainee who called his rifle a gun to run around and around the parade grounds, alternately thrusting his weapon aloft and slapping at his crotch yelling "This is my rifle, this is my gun! This is for fighting, this is for fun!"

Whenever we broke cadence and fell out of formation to "take 10!" we exercised our soldierly prerogatives to smoke and talk dirty. But first, we brushed our teeth.

We pulled collapsible toothbrushes from our shirt pockets countless times because they were part of a grand experiment. Soldiers, it had been discovered, had an inordinate amount of tooth decay. That was the case, the Army deduced, because trainees had poor oral hygiene. What would happen if trainees took exceptionally good care of their teeth? Would it not eliminate the time and money spent having those teeth yanked out or repaired? So we brushed and brushed and brushed, but never knew the results of our test.

When we weren't brushing, running, eating or sleeping, we were learning how to kill. We were taught the Army way to kill with knives, with clubs, with our hands, and using every type of semi-auto, full-auto weapon, with hand grenades, grenade launchers, disposable bazookas called LAWs, with mines and rockets. We learned it all quickly and often badly.

My excellent marksmanship, which had been my saving grace in basic, continued in AIT. I was shooting at expert level with every weapon, from the .45-caliber pistol to the .50-caliber M-2 Browning machine gun. So I was disgusted and royally pissed off when, on the morning of M-16 qualification day, I couldn't seem to hit a single target. The shit-eating thing kept jamming or spinning well-aimed shots into the dirt. I complained to the range cadre but was told to quit fucking whining and just shoot the best I could. I loudly cursed its sorry M-16 soul with each stoppage or miss. The drill sergeant and range master both grabbed the weapon, fired it and failed to hit anything. Then it jammed on them.

"Come with me, private," the range master said.

We walked to a huge shop truck at the back of the range.

"There's a gunsmith in there. Go fix your piece, Bub."

I opened the door and walked in to find a white-haired elf in civilian garb. His blue shirt sleeves were held up with garters, a green eyeshade was propped on his brow and wire-rimmed glasses perched on his red nose. He was surrounded by the tools of his trade. I handed "Santa" the offending M-16.

"Aw, let's see here," the gunsmith said. He deftly disassembled the rifle and replaced his spectacles with an eyepiece. "Aw, ummm, buffer, tube 'n' spring, Boy-Howdy! Bolt carrier... gad! The thing's got upper and lower receiver problems." He reached into a cabinet and took out plastic bags holding new buffer bits, and refitted or rebuilt the whole rear of the rifle. Sitting on a stool, quietly watching and occasionally handing tools or small parts to the gentleman was the most pleasant half an hour I'd spent in the Army.

I stepped out of the gunsmith's fluorescent world into the late afternoon sun grasping my tuned-up rifle. It was quiet. Most of my company had qualified and were riding back to chow. I had to stick around and try again, re-shooting with several others, mostly the do-it-again-better "bolos."

We were set up in the middle of the firing line, dozens of empty foxholes to our left and right. My turn came. Wrapping the rifle sling around my forearm, I started popping away. Four magazines, ten rounds each. Behind me, sitting in what resembled a white school desk, was another private, keeping my score.

One after another, the silhouette targets popped up. One after another, I shot 'em down. I wasn't counting, just fixing on targets, feeling the smoothly operating weapon at work in my hands. Before long, I became aware of a small crowd gathering behind the scorekeeper. Among the observers was my CO, Capt. Little and the range master. They were bobbing their helmeted heads over my chart.

They walked away as the last target fell. The scorekeeper complimented me and said I'd shot a 39 outta 40. I shouldered my reborn firearm and climbed up into the truck that was waiting for us last shooters.

Just before the driver turned the ignition key, the CO walked up to the tailgate of the truck. "Do you people know who shot the best in the battalion today? Pvt. Myers."

With a chorus of "way to go dickhead" ringing in my ears, I beamed all the way back to the barracks.

I had fun with all the weapons, except for grenades. I loathed them.

Grenade training began in a pit, the hard walls of which were scarred by grenades that had exploded before they could make it over the wall. As I practiced tossing a few dummy grenades, the instructor told stories about trainees who had been blasted by grenades they had dropped. Then he handed a "baseball" grenade to me and I positioned myself to throw it.

"Prepare to pull!" the sergeant said.

I assumed the proper hands-at-chest-level stance and put a finger through the pin.

"Pull pin!"

I yanked out the pin.

"Jesus Christ! Get down!" the sergeant yelled. He grabbed my shoulders and shoved me to the ground. There was an eardrum-jarring explosion.

A trainee in the next pit, not waiting for the throw command, simply lobbed his grenade a mere three feet over the concrete wall. Every sergeant from a mile around came in and shit down the neck of the impatient trainee. Soon the instructor was back to me. I was standing with my live grenade clenched tightly waiting for the command to throw.

"To hell with that idiot and this bullshit," the sergeant said, abandoning his by-the-book approach. "Just throw that grenade." I tossed it. Dropped down. It exploded. Now, I was ready for the combat grenade course.

That course, overlooked by four observation towers, had us running and dodging through some trees and log piles, ending at a log-and-sandbag roofless bunker.

"All right, prepare to move, you people," commanded a voice from a tower loudspeaker. Our rifles slung over our shoulders, we stood fidgeting in line. When the time came, we were handed two live baseball grenades. One by one, we dashed down the trail, following orders barked from the tower. Using the trees and logs as cover, each man finally flung himself behind a larger barricade and threw his grenades, one at a time, toward the bunker.

It was my turn.

"Go!"

I ran behind one tree.

"Go!"

I scurried to a log pile.

"Go!"

I ran to another tree.

"Go!"

I ran again, hit the dirt and, not waiting for a command, rolled over and pulled out the pins ... on both grenades. Confidence was high! Then I felt my fuck-up meter jump to crucial. My confusion turned to fear. I was lying there squeezing down the spoons on two live grenades. "Goddamn!" boomed the loudspeaker voice. "Uh, trainee! What the hell did you do? OK, git up! OK ...Throw yr' right hand grenade only! ... Now!"

I stood and pitched the little bomb lamely. It landed halfway to the target bunker as I ducked down.

Boom!

"OK ...Recover! ... Private! Hold that spoon tight ... Do not let go of that spoon. Slowly now, with your right hand grab the grenade and spoon together ...OK!"

Flushed and flustered, I threw the grenade, but it too fell sadly short of the target. My ears were still reverberating from the blasts as I exited the course into the harshest verbal assault of my life. Every person of higher rank was in my face.

"Godfuckingdamn, if that wasn't the stupidest stunt I've ever seen!" "Never come on my range again, private." "For a big fuckbag you sure can't throw very goddamn far." "What's the matter with you? You got a profile for no fucking brains?"

That considerable lapse of common sense on the grenade course, right on the heels of my moment of triumph with the M-16, was galling. And it didn't help my ego to fail my first attempt at the infantry proficiency test.

The daylong exam included oral quizzes and hands-on weaponry tests. It covered most of what we'd studied since basic, everything we'd written in copious notes as we stood in the field or sat in classrooms. For a week before the exam, the drill sergeants spent evening hours in the barracks, prepping us by asking questions. What was the treatment for a sucking chest wound? What was the kill radius of a particular type of land mine? How do you clear stoppages on an M-60? During the test, I missed a few of the first-aid questions. Learning to treat wounds was perversely less interesting than learning to cause them, and I would have readily admitted to daydreaming during some of the medics' lessons.

What did me in was mishandling the M-79 grenade launcher test. My problem was trying to outguess the Army. I was loading the weapon properly, then instantly decided that I had to be wrong, because it seemed too easy. They had taught us a confabulated procedure that was meant to keep us from damaging our thumbs from the '79s recoil. I took that Army method, turned it on its head and fucked it all up. I was fumbling frantically hand-over-hand trying to load the thing when the sergeant who was giving the test shook his head and told me to give up.

I felt sick to my soul about what was another in a line of failures.

Two days after 11 of us flunked the test, I took it again. As I stood in formation, I wanted to fade into the ranks of the 100 men who were about to take it for the first time. The last thing I wanted was any attention drawn to myself.

"Myers, you big bastard!" bellowed a voice from in front of the formation.

I'd been spotted by one of the training center honchos, Sgt. Maj. Major. (That was really his last name.) He'd been the first sergeant in my first basic company.

"Glad to see you made it into the infantry, Myers!"

"Hello, top sergeant," I answered through gritted teeth. I stiffened my body to keep it from melting with the flush of embarrassment into the gravel. But I recovered sufficiently to get everything pretty much right that day, and scored perfectly on the M-79 test.

Escape and Evasion

A pine forest was the classroom for a test called escape and evasion. The task: Sneak in the dark, unarmed, through enemy lines.

The escape part was implied, with the evading beginning at 21:00 on a chilly, windless night. The exercise was preceded by a strange bit of theater starring a chunky cadre sergeant holding a rabbit in his left hand. It was a white bunny, a scared bunny. From where I sat in the bleachers, I could see it twitch.

"When you people are out in the jungle, you gotta prepare to eat anything," the sergeant said. "Do you understand me? Anything to stay alive."

He spoke for 30 minutes about survival, his voice booming out past the floodlights into the cold air. "... and there's only one way to survive. You gotta kill and you gotta kill quick. Like you're gonna kill ol' Charles. You're gonna kill him and you're gonna hafta kill him quick. And kill other things too, just so's to survive."

Without disturbing the rhythm of his speech, he grasped the rabbit with both hands, twisted its head and ripped its skin down and off. Then he tore off the legs and pulled the guts out. He threw the parts at the soldiers in the stands. One leg flew past me and landed in the lap of a skinny soldier who eyed it queasily and asked, "Good God, what am I supposed to do with this?"

"Buddy up into four- or five-man squads, people," shouted the bloody-fingered sergeant. "Your objective is to out-think, out-maneuver and out-last the bad people who are out to get you. Now move out, make this safe, make this happen!"

We climbed down from the bleachers, assembled at the edge of the field and, at the blow of a whistle, fanned out into the woods—the skinny fellow still clutching the rabbit's leg.

The four trainees with me included an enthusiastic 17-year-old enlistee who acted as scout for awhile. We soon discovered how easy it was to get separated from each other, so we stopped letting him go ahead.

The woods were infested with men. We could never be sure which were evaders and which were trainee "enemy." So we did our best to avoid everyone. We didn't know what would happen to us if we were captured, but we'd heard enough horror tales about the fate of prisoners—and enough lectures about not giving any information (just name, rank, serial number) to the enemy—not to want to find out.

We also weren't sure how far it was to our destination, but we knew we would have to cover several miles at least. One of our few points of reference was a highway to our right, which we'd been ordered not to use as a path to safety. The two-lane blacktop shone in the light of the fat moon that slipped in and out of the clouds.

In less than two hours, we'd made our way through the forest, scooting away from noise and muffled words all around us. We emerged at the edge of a grassy 40-yard-wide power line path that bisected the escape-and-evasion territory. There were more people in the vicinity than ever. Many of them, I knew, were enemy troops straining to glimpse us would-be evaders. Those clowns hoped to capture us and drag us off to the compound that glowed in the darkness a quarter-mile down the trace. We had no idea how to get across that open space without being seen.

"Halt! Stop right there!" The five of us heard the order, turned and saw a rifle-toting profile not far down the edge of the power line path. We fought the instinct to freeze and dashed back in the direction we'd come from.

Along with the sound of our hearts pumping, we could hear several pursuers.

We backtracked for five minutes—it seemed much longer—until there were no more sounds of boots crunching through the underbrush behind us.

As we stopped to catch our breath, we also caught sight of the forbidden highway through the trees. We looked at it, then at each other. After a little whispered debate, we decided to make a beeline for the highway. Sure it was officially off limits. But we were damned if we were going to try to cross that treeless stretch again—not with that survival lecture so fresh in our minds.

The five of us crawled single-file in the ditch along the highway, incessantly glancing up the bank for the enemy. We saw a lot of them, especially as we approached the intersection of the power line path and the highway. We managed to slink by undetected, then quickened our pace. No one seemed to be lurking in the second section of the forest and there was no traffic on the highway.

It was well after midnight when we spotted two buses to our left. I stood and headed cautiously toward them. "Is this the pickup place?" I asked of a driver, who was leaning on the front of the first bus, his arms folded.

"Yeah," the driver replied as he reached through the open door and grabbed a clipboard from his seat. He wrote down my name and those of the four men who'd walked up behind me. Then he told us we might as well get some sleep. It would be a couple of hours before the buses headed back to the barracks.

We stretched out in the brown grass, zipped our field jackets up to our necks for warmth and, using our arms as pillows, snoozed until we heard the mumbled bitching and moaning of the slowly growing crowd, followed by the ignition of the buses.

By using the highway, we'd made good time and had been the first to arrive at the pickup point. Eventually, about 80 percent of the trainees joined us. The unlucky 20 percent had been, for the most part, the first ones to reach the grass trace and had kept the enemy busy molesting them while the rest of us slipped past.

The last week of AIT was taken up by field training exercises. FTX provided the closest thing to warfare conditions that infantry trainees experienced. The whole company saddled up its field kit and marched for miles to a wooded area. In the chill and spotty rain of late October, we began digging the first in a series of two-man fighting positions that would serve as our temporary sleeping quarters and "foxholes" for the next few nights. We were wearing our wet weather gear and helmets, laboring over shovels and mattocks, when whistles blew. We were told to fall our sorry butts into formation.

A stuffy-nosed first lieutenant addressed us.

"I want to announce to you people that, as of January 2, the new Commander in Chief of the United States Armed Forces will be Richard Milhouse Nixon." A subdued groan rippled through the soggy ranks.

"All right, that's enough. Now you slack-jawed nut-munchers get back to work," the drill sergeant barked. "You've had e-fucking-nough of a break."

We were re-excavating the pits worked over by all the preceding FTX companies. But those lightweights hadn't dug deep enough, so there was still plenty of earth to be moved. To make the digging easier and to keep our weapons clean, Lockhart and I did what we'd been told a good soldier never did—we leaned our rifles just out of reach. We'd been digging side by side for half an hour after the presidential formation when shadows suddenly darkened our dig.

An honest-to-god brigadier general, a light colonel and our company captain loomed over us. We came to attention in our wretched hole, gazing squarely at the general's belt.

The general spoke. "Trainees, pretend we're the enemy and we're here to kill you. What are you going to do?"

We stood stupified.

"Aren't you going to grab your weapons?"

We lunged. Before we touched our M-16s, the general struck our helmets with his "swagger stick," aka a dead branch. Tap, tap.

"You two are dead. I want you two trainees to lay there being dead, thinking about what just happened here ... Do you understand?"

"Yes sir."

Then he and the others turned away, shunning us. Lockhart and I, our faces pressed into the damp brown earth, heard Capt. Little address our drill sergeant.

"I want those two people to lay there until they start growing roots in the dirt, sergeant."

"Yes, sir!"

Twenty-some minutes passed, during which our drill sergeant heaped verbal abuse on our cringing forms. After what seemed ample time to contemplate our sin, Lockhart meekly asked, "Uh, drill sergeant, are we dead enough yet?" –

"Yeah, you two idiots better get back to work."

Following that first cold night in our damp fighting positions, we roused to a misty, cold day. The trial awaiting us was the daytime assault course. We marched to a forested collection spot where each squad crammed into a windowless, armored personnel carrier, then raced full-tilt over a rough track, rattling and crashing around before lurching to a stop.

We piled out, dizzily fell in and formed up. Blank ammo magazines were issued and, to the sound of loud shouts and trilling whistles, we scrambled up a dusty, sharp incline. During the assault, we zigzagged from firing barricade to firing barricade. We'd stop briefly to blaze away at pretend targets then jump back up and on to the next position. When we reached the top, we were panting and sweating from our helmets to our boots. We dropped, spent, onto bleacher seats and watched the next wave of soldiers "fight" their way uphill.

The rest of FTX was a blur of battle drills, field craft trials, ambushes, counter-ambushes, patrolling and concentrated discomfort.

The next night, we were attacked by shadowy "aggressors" and had to shift positions and retrench in the darkness. Morning came and we did a cordon and search of an "enemy village," flushing aggressors from huts, tunnels and bunkers. Our company failed the compass reading course but did fine in map reading and fending off the pretend aggressors. Finally, there was the much anticipated live fire exercise. We were told to form a line that would pivot from a point at the far left, advancing from the brushy base of the hill. We were to rake the hill and its targets with live ammunition until we swept over the crest.

It was crucial that we stay "shoulder to shoulder" and not step ahead or fall behind each other. We were positioning up when our drill sergeant called me over. "Myers, I want you staying right beside Pvt. Phillips here. You see he keeps up and on line with us. You see he controls his weapon. You see he doesn't shoot nobody. You understand?"

Phillips had recycled in late to my platoon. He was short, had a slack mouth and a swarthy chin shadow and greasy hair. I'd seen some curious duds in the special training battalion, but this guy was the foldout beauty of that magazine. He couldn't count simple cadence, pull his guard alone or even lace and tie his own boots.

"Buddy-up with Phillips!? Shit noooo!" My mind screamed.

"Yes, drill sergeant," I replied.

Phillips and I were placed at the pivot point where we wouldn't have to cover much ground. I was right next to him. Almost touching. Other men in our platoon were spread yards apart with white-helmeted range cadres interspersed among them. Drill sergeants watched our backs.

With manly shouts and shrieking whistles, the assault began. M-16s were rattling away as the company line hit the first firing positions. It was on. Phillips' feet caught sideways in a root gnarl and he fell. I tripped trying to pull him up, putting us behind our comrades. The two of us struggled into our first firing position and started blasting away. Phillips spun sideways and looked at me, his finger still on the trigger, spraying live rounds over my head. I thrust my arm at his swinging rifle. As I did, he fell backward over a stump. His M-16 dropped, clattering on the ground. Phillips snatched it, stood looking uphill and, without a glance at me, resumed firing.

I was so goddamned busy yelling at and trying to deal with Phillips and my own entangled feet that I hadn't fired a round. In less than two minutes, WD was back. He could see the exasperation on my sweating face and said, "Never gonna work out." Then he grabbed Phillips, separated him from his weapon, ordered me to continue up the course and Phillips to get out of the line. I double-timed to catch up with the others, get back on line and finish the assault.

Phillips disappeared that night.

It rained each day of FTX. We were cold and wet at night, warm and damp in the day. Our rubberized rain gear ripped from overuse. We left our soggy boots on our swelling feet for fear we couldn't get them back on.

On the last day, the sun came out. It made our field jackets and fatigues steam from damp and sweat as we geared up and watered up (two canteens) for the march back to our barracks. There were 17 3/4 miles of up and down pain between us and the company area. After the first five miles, we were hurting but all accounted for. At the 10-mile point, everyone was cramping and dragging but still there. Two field ambulances trailed our strung-out column, treating and resurrecting those falling by the way.

Nine guys were out in front. I was 50 yards behind them, my poor feet pistoning up and down. Being that close to the lead inspired me to keep slogging. My feet began sending last-gasp messages to my brain, but I knew that every muscle in my lower body would contract mercilessly if I stopped.

I glanced to my right and saw a guy I didn't recognize trying to pass me. Neither of us had enough energy for theatrics, so sprinting ahead was out of the question. We sized up each other and found nothing special, just two ratty looking GIs. So we both kept putting one foot in front of the other, hitting the road with our boots in a plodding rhythm. We glanced at each other constantly, straining to find a weakness, a gradual slowing of pace, something. We stayed in lockstep.

After about three miles of slow-motion foot racing, I pulled ahead. My challenger conceded defeat and began falling farther behind. I finally got within 15 feet of the leaders and was one of the first dozen men to reach the barracks, three-plus hours after we had begun the march.

After depositing my rifle in the weapons locker, I plopped onto my bunk and peeled off my boots. My feet began to crumple toes-to-heel, trying to make fists, while ballooning far larger than their usual size thirteen. To keep the swelling down, and the muscles from balling up, I rubbed them vigorously with my Zippo lighter for an hour before aiming them in the direction of the chow line.

The next morning, we were relishing the thought of a weekend off base.

But before we could go, we had to clean the weapons we'd brought back from FTX. I spent an hour taking apart, brushing, oiling and Q-tip-swabbing, then reassembling my M-16 with the kind of care it takes to get a classic car shining and purring. I was the first to hand a rifle to WD for inspection. The drill sergeant eyed it carefully. "Good, speedy job, Myers. Out-fuckin'-standing."

I went back to my locker and put on a white turtleneck and peace symbol on a chain—both newly acquired at the PX—and my other civilian clothes. Then I joined the horde of similarly spiffy dudes who were waiting for the bus to Seattle.

We spent a day and a half exploring the wharf, haunting downtown bars and knocking back beers in our rooms at the inauspicious Mayflower Motel. We enjoyed the sight of all those people wearing colors other than olive green.

The enemy is us

Monday brought a different shade of green: Kelly. It was the color of the uniforms of the FTX aggressor. Lockhart, I and about 20 others from our company were chosen to be enemy participants in the week's upcoming war games.

We excited "bad guys" reported to company supply for our uniforms: smocks that laced up and roomy pants with button-up flies. Then it was on to the armorer for blank suppressed M-14 rifles. We grabbed our web gear and hopped into the waiting trucks. We were driven to an oppressive-looking, nearly hidden valley in which a huge cook tent sat spouting greasy smoke. Around it were several equally large tents that served as headquarters and barracks.

The tents had wooden floors and air mattresses, which made sleeping much more comfortable than when we were the FTX "good guys" in foxholes. Not that we got much sleep over the next few days. That first afternoon, I was among enemy troops holding a "ville" that was being searched by trainees. Somehow, the numbnut trainees neglected to clear the makeshift building where I was waiting to pounce. I let them pass me, then jumped out the door blazing away at a crowd of them with my M-14. I killed four before the survivors flanked me and gunned me down. It was good fun.

At 02:00 the next morning, a half dozen of us were roused from sleep and trucked near the base of a sopping wet hill. We were told to attack a platoon of trainees who were entrenched on the top. The bogus commando raid took place in a noisy rain. We felt sorry for ourselves as we slogged through the trees. But we were not quite as miserable as our hapless prey, who we found huddled over a wretched fire, trying to heat coffee. I pitied them. A week earlier, I'd been in their boots, unable to get desperately needed sleep in a flooded foxhole.

I snuck up on a trainee who was hunched in his poncho near the fire, hands shoved into his pockets for warmth. When he saw me, he started to reach for his rifle, then gave a to-hell-with-it shrug and stood up.

"Bang, bang," I said stupidly. "I'm an aggressor."

My victim merely walked away and joined the other prisoners, who were starting to pack their soaked gear and move out.

Daylight brought a more serious game.

Somebody who was cycling through FTX figured his outfit's dud, a big guy who had been recycled once or twice, needed to be taught yet another lesson. "Fuck him over good," was the way I heard it. So they rigged one of their patrols, putting the poor dud on point and arranging for everyone else to disappear and let us aggressors capture him.

I was smoking and joking with some of my fellow bad guys when several other company aggressors who were billeted in the big tent across the road paraded single file into camp leading a bound captive. I watched them remove the rope that bound the dud's hands and heard them order him to strip to his shorts. They then shoved him into a pit.

Curious, my friends and I walked over to the hole. It was at least 12 feet deep, and dug so that a man couldn't easily climb out of it. The dud was curled into a corner, shivering. Even if there had been sunshine, it wouldn't have reached his nearly naked body. His light blond, short-cropped hair blended with his pasty complexion, giving him the look of a six-foot gnome.

While we looked on, the handful of captors started tormenting the poor bastard. They brought trays of mixed chow, open cartons of milk and juice from the mess tent and dumped and drizzled it all on his head. The guy started spinning wildly about the pit, screaming, froth flying from his mouth. Then they kicked dirt into the pit. Some were about to make good on threats to piss on him when I and Lockhart with a couple of others said, "Leave him be." A couple of staff sergeants in the crowd told us to mind our own fucking shit. We groaned and walked off. We'd had enough of that whole scene.

The moans from the dud were sounding weak and desperate when we returned from another wet, middle-of-the-night attack. Lockhart and I had just hopped off the truck's tailgate and were hanging our weapons on the rack inside our tent when we heard a stomach-churning sound coming from the next tent. We crept close to its open flap and peered in. We could see the dud dangling half naked and upside down with his knees bent over some sort of pole contraption. There were wires clamped to his chest. One of the sergeants interrogating him intermittently cranked a little generator, which sent current pulsing through the wires. One guy smacked him back and forth across his face, demanding that he name his company commander. The prisoner only moaned and screamed some more.

The torturers wore the expressions of kids who delighted in pulling legs off insects.

Lockhart and I looked at each other, eyes wide with disgust. We turned in, somehow managing to nod off. At 05:00, I was jostled awake by WD, who growled, "Come with me." I grabbed my rifle and followed the sergeant to the tent where the dud had been strung up two hours ago. Before we walked inside, WD spoke.

"We're going to guard these prisoners this morning. Let's wake these stupid fuckers up." There were five prisoners, including the dud. They were huddled into fetal positions. WD started prodding them with his feet. "Get up, you bastards, get up now!" All five were shivering as they began to straighten their bodies. "You're cold?" the sergeant asked. "All right then, get up, get running."

They jogged pitifully around and around and around inside the tent, their bare feet slapping and sometimes slipping on the cold floorboards. I stood there at port arms, ashamed and confused.

"You cocksuckers warm yet?" WD would ask from time to time. "No? Well, keep'a going."

At 07:00, the reveille whistle blew into the morning's fog. FTX was over. The drill sergeant left the tent. Another entered, carrying a duffel bag. "OK, you dicks, here's your boots," he said to the former prisoners. "Fall out. Breakfast'll be here in, oh, 15-20 minutes." The men looked at him with glazed eyes. "C'mon, get up, fall out. Bacon, eggs and everything... hot food for ya."

The sergeant marched out. I watched the five sit there, struggling to get their boots onto their swollen feet. Not one of them looked at or spoke to me. They walked out of the tent, free men.

I heard someone tell the former prisoners they had just enough time to get through the chow line before their company would arrive to pick them up. They filled their plates and sat silently in a corner of the mess tent. One of them, I heard, was a buck sergeant who'd been busted to E-1 for breaking during the interrogation and naming his company commander.

Following our breakfast, we "bad guys" policed the camp and threw our tired butts and wet gear into the back of a truck for the ride to our company area. I was quiet, exhausted, disgusted. I'd been knocked around and hassled and pretty much treated like shit the last few weeks but had never experienced anything like what they'd done to that dud. If that was the way the Army built men, I wasn't optimistic about my future in the military.

We'll take him from here

When we returned to the barracks, we were told to keep wearing our damp, ripe, aggressor outfits because we were going out that night to be "bad guys" during Escape and Evasion. After dark, we were taken to the lane that bisected the Escape and Evasion area.

We formed up to hear our instructions and orders. "You will aggressively patrol this area looking for these people," a sergeant told us. "You will capture not kill them. Do not use excessive force. If you must bust a head, or nuts, or bust anything, they'd better be killing your ass. Do you understand? Do not butt-strike anyone and all bayonets will remain here. Do you understand!?"

"Yes, drill sergeant!"

Lockhart and I took positions on one side of the grassy lane, opposite three other aggressors. We leaned against a tree and hid the glow of our cigarettes, as much to avoid the wrath of the roaming sergeants as to keep the enemy from spotting us. After an hour, we heard rustling. Four or five evaders were about to enter the road.

"Halt!" I yelled. The evaders squealed and high-tailed it back into the woods. All except one—a buck sergeant who stumbled. Five of us grabbed him. We were pleased to find we'd caught a big fish, a training cadre from a headquarters company who was going through FTX with the troops.

"God, no," the captive said. "Goddamnit!"

Those were the only words he spoke, despite our insistence that he identify himself, his company, his commander. He didn't resist us, though.

"What are we going to do with this fucker?" Lockhart asked.

"Let's take his boots off," one of the others said. "And cover his face before we take him in." I thought that was a little strange, but went along with it. After all, I'd managed to avoid capture during Escape and Evasion. If this character couldn't do the same, well, he deserved whatever he got. That's war.

We took off his field jacket and put it on backward, with the hood pulled up to cover his face. We didn't put his arms in the jacket, using the sleeves instead to tie his hands behind his back. Then we tied his shoelaces together and strung his boots around his neck so they hung over his chest.

The five of us began to accompany the hapless sergeant, who we started out making walk backward, to the floodlit compound down the road. I proposed that Lockhart and I could handle the prisoner, and suggested the others see if they could snag more evaders. They agreed, and headed back into the dark.

If the Army had intended the Escape and Evasion compound to resemble a concentration camp, it had succeeded. Its several barracks-like gray buildings were surrounded by guard towers and barbed wire. The bare earth under the tower floodlights contrasted starkly with the lush conifer forest that outlined the compound.

Lights shone from the randomly placed windows. As we got closer, we could see movement inside. At the entrance, we were challenged by a guard.

"We've got a prisoner for you," I said.

"OK. We'll take him from here." The guards opened a screened door in the bigger gate and grabbed our prisoner, shutting the door behind him. Lockhart and I didn't get a receipt or even a nod.

The guard led the prisoner toward the buildings, which were less than 50 yards from where Lockhart and I stood gaping outside the barbed wire. We could hear repeated shouts in the distance, although we couldn't make out any words. All of the shadowy figures we glimpsed through open doors and windows were moving—except for one man, who was kneeling with his hands apparently tied behind his back.

The stories we'd heard about this place must have been more than rumors designed to frighten trainees. They really did beat you to make you tell your commander's name. Maybe they did strap you over a drum and tie thin wire across your mouth, like the guy who supposedly panicked and cut his mouth so badly an ambulance was called. Maybe they did use electrodes. Maybe they did tie naked guys to tree stumps—there were stumps in the compound—and toss freezing water on them.

Our increasingly horrible imaginings were disrupted by a drill sergeant who seemed to come from nowhere. He barked at me and Lockhart through the wire.

"You silly fuckers wanna be in here!? Just let me find you hangin' round in another five minutes, and I'll make yer dreams come true. Better to get your goddamned asses outta here."

"Yes, drill sergeant!"

As we left, I was thinking about the poor guy we'd delivered into more misery. "Piss on this," I said to Lockhart. "There's no fucking sense in putting people through that." Lockhart agreed.

We didn't rejoin the other aggressors, but spent the rest of the night hiding the glow from our cigarettes and letting evaders walk past.

My stint as an aggressor was the end of my training. After the Escape and Evasion episode, I spent a day catching up on sleep and helping police the barracks in preparation for the company's departure. I spent the final night on guard duty.

On the last morning, the graduating trainees filed into a base theater for ceremonies that included the presentation of awards. We would walk to the stage as a colonel distributed certificates for exemplary performance during AIT. I was paying only marginal attention until the colonel announced the next award was for the best marksman, the trainee who had made a nearly perfect score on the rifle range.

I was all ears. I shot a 39 ... Why didn't somebody tell me about this award?

"And the trainee who shot a 39 is ..." The name didn't register in my brain. I just knew it wasn't mine. "...and I'm sure that his father, General So-and-So, is very proud of him."

Oh. That explained it. I wasn't dejected. After all, I hadn't expected any recognition. But I was more ready than ever to leave Fort Lewis.

The afternoon's ceremonies on the parade field were the same as those of graduation from basic training, except this time we wore camouflage helmet covers and shouldered M-16s. After the ceremonies, I caught a bus to Sea-Tac and from there a plane home. My coat pocket bulged with tickets and orders—orders approving leave, orders telling me to report to Oakland Army Terminal, orders confirming my destination as RVN. Fourteen days in Boise was all that stood between me and the Republic of Vietnam.

Chapter 6: Kill those commies

It was a hi-there, bye-there, two-week leave. I drank beer (though still under legal age) with my friends and chowed down on Mom's fried chicken, fried okra, flaky biscuits, special spaghetti and fluffy mashed potatoes with, oh man, her meatloaf.

My brother Ken missed just about every dinner while I was home. Neither my folks nor I got more than a glimpse of him. He was like a ghost or comic super hero—popping in, popping out. Kenny was beginning a self-destructive bent that would plague him and us until his death. My little brother. His mission in life was to be as contrary as humanly possible. He was not malicious by nature but his behavior saddened my parents deeply. My going off to war was a drain on them, too. I felt crummy and helpless about that. We two were just a couple of shits.

My Army fatigues fit and felt better than anything hanging in my closet. My old jeans were a bit baggy and the old shirts seemed snug. But I was glad to be wearing civvies. The only time I had to put on my uniform while home was to report to the Mountain Home Air Base Military Pay Office where my final pre-Vietnam pay packet waited for me.

That morning, resplendent in my Army E-2 private's dress khakis, I hopped into our family's 1960 Plymouth station wagon. I drove down Vista Avenue and stopped in at the Phillips 66 station, which was owned by one of my dad's friends. "Fill'er up, Bill," I said. Bill popped open the hood, then walked back to the pumps muttering "How are you doing there, son? How's old Zeke?" not waiting for my reply.

There was one other customer, a middle-aged woman who was drinking a Coke while her big car was serviced by "the boy." She stood in the office, buttoned up in a tan, '50s-style mohair coat. She had on gray sneakers, sported vibrant red hair and had an oversized, jeweled American flag on her lapel. Bill went back out to tend to the station wagon. When he left, the redhead walked quickly up to me and grabbed a khaki shirt sleeve.

"I just want you to know that we're proud of you boys," she said, peering at me through her winged glasses. "You don't know this, but I'm a member of the John Birch Society. And I want you to know that we're not only proud of you, we're behind you all the way. We hope and pray that you'll be able to kill those commies and keep our country free."

"Uh, thanks," I said, taking a step toward the door. "You're goin' to Vietnam, aren't you?" she asked. I nodded. "Well, I just want to wish you good luck." I thanked her again, turned and got out to the car just as Bill was tightening the gas cap.

I was shaking my head over the crazy lady during the 50-mile drive to the air base. I was also thinking what a drag it would be to have to salute again. But it was late in the day and there was no one around to salute at the base. I collected a manila envelope at the barred pay window, cashed my check with the civilian clerk and pocketed the $96 that she handed me. It was two weeks' pay, more than enough for a week's worth of drinking before I had to climb, all over again, back into the starched uniform and start saluting again.

Chapter 7: Assembly line to Vietnam

I never felt more like a cipher than I did at Oakland Army Terminal, the funnel through which thousands of men poured each day on their way overseas.

As during training, there were countless stripes to please, countless orders to obey. But the atmosphere was less intense, less disciplined. There were far too many soldiers being processed in far too short a time for anyone to feel personally affronted by orders.

About 50 of us fell off the bus and into formation. We were led into a whirring, buzzing room full of barbers, from which we emerged crew-cut clean.

I was assigned to the same area with some of my AIT buddies. The billets were cinderblock and concrete buildings that towered six and seven stories high, each floor filled with hundreds of green and gray tiered bunks.

After we stowed our gear, we were ordered to line up, alphabetically, for processing. Like widgets on an assembly line, we stopped at various stations in various buildings to get shots, to answer questions on endless sheets of paper, to have passport photos taken. It was evening before all 2,000 of us fell back into formation, only to get back into more lines for chow. It was 21:00 before I was back at my bunk. Everyone was preparing to hit the sack when a voice rang out above the quiet conversation.

"Is there a Pvt. Grady Myers here?"

Hundreds of heads turned toward the doorway. I felt a chill.

"Right here, specialist."

The messenger walked through the sea of bunks.

"Pvt. Myers, they seem to have lost the majority of your pre-travel packet. You'll have to go through processing again. And you'd better hurry, because it closes in an hour."

I cursed silently, then headed for the stairs.

I reported to the first station.

"What are you doing here?" asked the clerk.

"They lost my records. I don't know what I'm supposed to do."

"OK. What's your name?"

"Myers, Grady C., US56629054."

"All right," the clerk said, apparently having found my name on one form in a stack at his elbow.

There were more forms, more questions. "What's your blood type? ... Have you ever had malaria? ... Did you get your shots? You did? When? Two hours ago? We don't have a record of them. Roll up your sleeve."

It was 23:30 before I was fully reprocessed. As I walked back in the foggy darkness, I was alone on the sidewalks that had teemed with uniformed bodies during the day. The only sounds were my footsteps.

Reveille came at 06:00. I joined the line at a huge mess hall. After a leisurely meal of pancakes, eggs and sausage, I became one speck in a massive formation. In front of the orderly throng was a story-high, white review stand. Officers stood behind a lectern and opened what appeared to be large ledger books.

They spoke into microphones, reading off names and assignments. As each man heard his name and serial number, he would report to the podium, pick up more orders and be told where to report next.

It was two hours before my name was called. I began to feel dizzy as the sun climbed higher, but stood straight and silent like nearly everyone else. One man in the formation, however, was having trouble maintaining decorum. He apparently found the situation hilarious. Or his nerves were frayed beyond containment. In either case, someone at a microphone took notice of one Pvt. Jackass.

"There's some laughing and noise out there. If there's any more of that, you people are going to be in a lot of trouble."

The soldier stifled his laughter. For awhile.

"NUTZ," sounded a voice over the loudspeaker. "Lowell J."

Upon hearing the mispronunciation that had plagued my AIT buddy, I grinned. Pvt. Jackass completely cracked up, bursting into guffaws that no one in formation could help but hear.

"I want to see that man right there!" rang the barely restrained voice of an officer.

A sergeant walked into the lines, hauled the offender to the front of the formation and ordered him to get into a push-up position.

Half an hour later, the speakers sounded with "Myers, Grady C., US56629054."

When I walked up to get my papers, I glanced down at the guy who had been laughing. His arms were straining, his brow was sweating and he definitely wasn't smiling.

I retrieved my gear from the concrete-block building and fell into yet another line and signed yet more papers. Then I picked up my clothing issue for Vietnam, jungle fatigues and boots, hats and T-shirts—all of it, even the boxer shorts, in olive drab.

I moved to the assigned area in what looked like the world's largest aircraft hangar. It had been partitioned with a maze of curtains and filled with bunks. I found my rack and took my first breather in a day and a half. After resting, I changed from khakis into my new fatigues. I felt awkwardly spiffy.

Embarkation time wasn't until the next evening, and I was pleased to hear that I was free to use the post facilities. Although many of my pals from training weren't there—some, like Lockhart, had volunteered for airborne and had gone to Fort Benning, Ga.—I found four cronies and headed for the bowling lanes, the only place we could think of that served beer.

We had the alley practically to ourselves and spent the day bowling poorly, talking loudly and drinking constantly. It was dark when we staggered back to the hangar and fell asleep.

Our rowdiness was gone in the morning. Most guys spent the remainder of their free time staring, reading and worrying. Everyone was uptight. The most involved conversation I heard that day was along the lines of, "Man, I want to get out of this place. What a hole!"

After supper, we were told to change back into our khakis. We donned field jackets and garrison caps, packed our duffel bags and boarded buses for California's Travis Air Force Base.

We got off the bus and stood around in the cavernous air terminal. Outside, a sleek Seaboard World Airlines stretch DC-8 waited for us. Nervousness was reaching a peak.

Someone tapped me on the shoulder. It was an AIT buddy.

"Look, look," he said. "Over there at the counter. It's Phillips."

Sure enough, it was the dud who had almost gunned me down. He must have been recycled and was heading somewhere else. He cast a shadow over our departure.

"Jesus Christ, what a bad omen," someone said. "I'm gonna die. That fucking Phillips is gonna kill me."

Phillips stood there beside an older woman—an aunt? a guardian?—and made his old platoon mates genuinely agitated. It was not rational to think Phillips would bring us bad luck, but this wasn't a moment in which logic reigned. We all quietly turned our backs to the counter and looked out at the jet.

"OK, let's go," someone said.

We tossed our duffel bags into luggage bins, walked out into the damp night air and climbed the boarding ramp.

It seemed a matter of seconds before the ramp was pulled up and the jet was off the ground. Although I sat on the aisle, I could peer out the window at the receding lights of Sacramento. Within minutes, the jet was over the Pacific.

In-country -

I'd been separated from my friends during boarding and ended up directly behind the cockpit, sitting beside two NCOs who were in command of the troops on the chartered flight. Because of my proximity to the men in charge, I felt compelled to be on better behavior than the guys in the back, who got a bit rowdy as soon as the wheels left the runway. I had to content myself with writing letters and eyeing the stewardesses, who stored their personal paraphernalia in a low compartment to the front and right of me. Throughout the flight, whenever one of the lovelies felt the need to powder her nose or touch up her mascara, she would have to bend over—and, in the process, place her mini-skirted bottom in the vicinity of my elbow. By the time the fourth stewardess stooped down, I knew exactly where to drape my arm so that it would be rubbed by the shapely derriere.

The stewardii, as I liked to think of them, spent most of their time dodging passes and passing out pillows. The pillows were used more for fighting than for sleeping as the nervous guys let off steam. They were shedding their shirts and their inhibitions. The commotion was too much for one of the NCOs sitting in the rear. He was a short, muscular Chicano with a drill sergeant's crest on his shirt. He started shoving people back into their seats and shouting at the top of his lungs.

"Straighten up and act like goddamn soldiers. What are you people doing?"

His language got abusive. He pushed a stewardess out of his way and, at that point, his bellowing became too much for the small, bespectacled master sergeant across the aisle from me.

The master sergeant, whose E-7 gave him the highest rank on the flight, put down the papers he'd been reading, walked over to the drill sergeant and said in a surprisingly gruff voice, "Sit your goddamn butt down in that seat and shut up, or I'm going to personally see that you're locked up in LBJ for a year."

At that, conversation was reduced to a murmur. We'd all heard about Long Binh Jail, the U.S. military prison in Vietnam.

All ears were waiting for the drill sergeant's reply. We didn't wait long. He told the master sergeant where to go, and that was the start of a good five minutes of arguing and cussing. When the smoke cleared, the drill sergeant was in his seat, fuming but quiet.

When the master sergeant strode back up the aisle, a cheer went up and pillows were tossed in the air. The reaction must have humiliated the drill sergeant even more, but he said nothing.

The plane stopped in Honolulu. We got to stretch our legs.

It was still daylight there, the temperature was a balmy 75. I was impressed with the lush landscape I'd seen on the approach to the islands and that everyone in the terminal looked so ... so Hawaiian. Their tanned, tropical skin made me feel more winter pale and pasty.

In 30 minutes, we were back in the air. I resumed letter-writing, which relaxed me, and scrawled postscript after postscript. I explained my nervousness in a letter to my friend Mueller: "The war makes us uneasy, scared and a little silly. We know some of us aren't coming back and that some will be maimed for the rest of our lives."

In a few hours, we landed at the Strategic Air Command terminal in Guam. It was warmer than Hawaii. I bought a Coke and CornNuts and watched a new shift of stewardesses board the jet. They were less attractive than the first four. I wondered if the prettier ones refused to sign waivers to fly into Nam.

It was the second evening of our long day when we arrived at Tan Son Nhut airfield outside Saigon. When the jet door swung open, it let in a blast of hot air. When I stepped outside, I felt as if a damp blanket had been thrown over me. The earth had a deep, musky odor that was unlike anything carried on the sea breezes of California, Hawaii and Guam.

The huge terminal was more like a hangar than a civilian airport facility. It buzzed with thousands of people in what seemed to be hundreds of different uniforms. We stood in a ragged formation for our baggage. When it appeared at the counter, we were marched to four green buses that were waiting, engines gunning, around a corner of the terminal. Between the buses were jeeps, each armed with an M-60 machine gun and two military policemen.

We craned our necks to catch our first glimpses of Vietnam through the steel mesh that covered the open bus windows. We could see row after row of military huts, soldiers of every description, jeeps, tanks and trucks. As they headed for the base at Long Binh, we saw more Asian faces and civilian vehicles, especially small motorcycles that wove in and out of the military traffic.

Above it all, helicopters came and helicopters went. For the next week, I would wake up and doze off to the noise of blades chopping the air.

Chapter 8: Anywhere but the 4th

We were taken to the 90th Replacement Depot at Long Binh, an Army enclave surrounded by barbed wire, gun emplacements, towers and searchlights. The reception center was a miniature version of Oakland Army Terminal, but instead of multi-story buildings, the processing took place in long, wall-less structures with only roofs. Partitions lit by fluorescent bulbs were scattered about. A loud-speaker voice told us where to form lines and which forms to pull from cubbyholes under long, high tables. I was getting expert at filling out forms, so this stuff was no sweat. From where I stood, I could see barracks and, in front of them, NCOs in their underwear, drinking beer. The bluish glow of television screens shone through the windows. Above the din of the reception center, I could make out the theme from the TV show "Combat."

On the way to our own barracks, we encountered soldiers with their own theme song: "Short, We're Short!" They were short-timers, their Date of Estimated Return from Overseas close at hand. Or, at least, they wanted us replacements—who faced a year in Vietnam before our DEROS—to feel bad. When a soldier stepped onto Vietnamese soil, he was shorter than the man getting off the plane behind him.

I couldn't see the men who were taunting us. It was after midnight. The pitch dark interspersed with glaring field lights silhouetted us as we entered our barracks. I stripped to my shorts, climbed behind a drapery of mosquito netting and lay sweltering on a bunk.

When the lights went out moments later, the barracks were illuminated by the soft red and green glow of flares being sent off outside the base. They would hang in the sky before floating down. I could hear helicopters and, in the distance, machine gun fire. The sound of Glenn Campbell singing "Wichita Lineman" drifted from someone's tape deck or radio. It was a strange lullaby, but it worked.

In the morning, we put on crisp fatigues and fell into a formation of what appeared to be thousands of soldiers. We listened as names were called and men were assigned to different units throughout Vietnam. I didn't hear my name.

The men remaining in formation were assigned chores, ranging from KP to ditch digging. My row was tapped to accept equipment from men who were passing through Long Binh on their way back to the U.S.

They were tough-looking troops, the men who formed a line to hand over their helmets and helmet liners, canteens and canteen covers, web belts and the rest of their combat gear. Although they wore reasonably clean uniforms, they provided quite a contrast to the replacements. Our uniforms bore no insignia and our boots were unscuffed.

They had the look of old-timers, which we at first tried to cultivate, then found impossible to avoid.

The line of men on their way back to "The World" snaked past. They were quiet. I wondered why guys who were so short weren't exuberant. I took their gas masks, methodically handing each one to another replacement, who peeled off its cover and pitched it into a bin.

The tempo of the procedure was interrupted by a visit from a brigadier general.

He wore his Army baseball cap with a black star on it. He was a hawk-nosed, tall man with a protruding Adam's apple. He looked to weigh all of 130 pounds as he went down the line, grasping hands of new and old troops. He walked up to me and held out his hand.

"Hello, son, where are you from? Boizee? Wonderful town!"

Then it was on to the next soldier and the next. Two aides followed behind, taking notes.

"From Dubuque? Wonderful, wonderful ... Cleveland? Good city, Cleveland ...

"How are you, son?"

The general moved on and I got back to processing gas masks—maybe 800 in all.

That night, I joined a stream of GIs who crammed into the barn-like EM club filled with hundreds of soldiers. That night it also held an awful Vietnamese band—the only recognizable song they played was "Hey Jude"—and two skinny Asian go-go girls. I sat down with some buddies at the bar, which ran the length of the club, and drank for an hour before heading back to the barracks.

My name wasn't called during the next morning's formation, nor was my row picked for any kind of duty. So I headed back to the barracks, where another soldier and I were discussing our possible fates when a sergeant walked in.

"Hey, I need a couple of guys to go with me to the garbage dump 'n' be security," he said. "You guys'll need to draw some weapons if ya do."

It was an order, not a request, but we were more than happy to comply. Maybe we would see some action. But, just as we were about to get some rifles, the sergeant changed his mind.

"Naw, forget it. We won't go today."

I was disappointed. I couldn't imagine what there would be to do at the dump, but now I had nothing to do except visit the PX.

With my buddy-for-the-day, I headed for the exchange in the noontime heat. First stop was one of the snack bars that were scattered around the base, where we bought Cokes from a Vietnamese couple who wore McDonald's-type paper hats. We sipped the drinks as we walked, taking in the rough-and-tumble, mining-camp atmosphere of Long Binh. An amazing mixture of civilians and military people scurried about in a kaleidoscope of costumes. Green Berets chatted with Air Force colonels, laundry women argued with clerks.

The large PX contained nearly everything I could've imagined in a stateside drugstore, and one thing I couldn't have—the most beautiful woman in the world.

Clear, fair skin; lustrous, long black hair ... She must have been a blend of French and Vietnamese. She was a clerk at the camera counter, where she glided about in her silk ao-dais, a tight native tunic of gun metal blue. I figured she'd been put there as eye candy to lure suckers such as myself into buying Kodak and Pentax cameras. I stayed in the next aisle, pretending to examine the selection of toothpaste, and ogled her until I had my fill.

My name wasn't called during that evening's formation, or the next morning's.

As I stood listening to the drone of names, I wondered which unit awaited me. Would I be sent to the Mekong Delta or the Highlands? Would I be with the 1st Infantry Division, aka the Big Red One? Or the 1st Cavalry Division, the 25th Infantry Division, the 173rd Airborne Brigade, the 101st Airborne Division, or maybe the Americal Division? It didn't much matter to me, as long as I wasn't sent to the 4th Infantry Division. I associated the 4th with the stories of boredom and horror told by my cadre in basic. It was, Jim Beam had said, a lousy outfit. An assignment with the 4th would be a sentence of death or, at least, a year on death row.

My third morning at Long Binh was spent on a road crew, breaking up a tarmac road with picks, then digging a ditch across it. After lunch, I fell into yet another formation, fully expecting to spend another afternoon laboring or girl-watching.

I was almost shocked when I heard my name. And I was almost sick when, as I ran from formation to the designated spot, I realized I'd been assigned to the 4th Infantry.

I had 45 minutes to gather my gear and to report to one side of the huge parade ground for transportation to Pleiku.

The parade ground, where about 20 of us threw down our gear, was a sea of rocks ranging in size from large to gargantuan. We were looking around for a comfortable place to sit and wait when a jeep pulled up. A lieutenant jumped out and told us the flight north had been postponed.

"You're due to take off tomorrow at 09:00," he said.

"Where are you going to billet us tonight?" someone asked.

"I'm afraid we're full up. The bunks that you left are now being filled. You'll have to spend the night here."

"Here on these damned rocks?"

But the officer hadn't heard the question or the complaints that followed. He was off in his jeep, presumably on his way to comfortable barracks and comfy local bunnies. We began rearranging rocks, trying to make reasonably smooth spots to spread our bedrolls. Everyone kept tossing rocks into the next guy's area and, before long, we gave up in disgust and headed en masse for the EM club to spend the rest of the day. We were tipsy in an hour, decidedly intoxicated in two and rip-snorting drunk in four. When we returned to our bed rocks. I addressed one of my drinking buddies:

"This is goddamn disgusting," I proclaimed, "I'm gonna show you what I'm gonna do, goddamnit."

I headed for the area on the parade ground where I'd stood in formation time and again. I was picturing the fat sergeant who always walked crunch-crunch-crunch over the rocks to a spot in front of a podium and called everyone to attention. Throughout each formation, the sergeant—who was growing progressively more hateful in my besotted mind—would stand there and mete out punishment to anyone he deemed was misbehaving, such as anyone who wore a smirk or a hat that was askew.

I knew exactly where the sergeant would stand the next morning and I counted paces to reach the spot. One, two, three, four steps, turn and stop. One, two, three, four, turn and stop. I staggered through the paces, bent over and, with a flourish, heaved my ever-loving guts out. I was proud of myself. My audience applauded. I stumbled back to my gear and fell asleep on the rocks.

A chorus of moans greeted the morning sun. We dragged our gear and bodies into a waiting bus for the drive back to Tan Son Nhut. Once in the terminal, we milled around and drank soda or sat and groaned, depending on the state of our hangovers.

"Everybody for Pleiku, on your feet," someone announced. "Let's go."

We shouldered our bags and walked to a C-123, a moderately large cargo plane with no seats. "All right, keep moving," someone behind me yelled. "We can park about 120 of you people in here if you'll back up." There was much shoving and scooting. "All right," one Air Force crewmen said when the shoving stopped. "Make yourselves comfortable." There was no chance of that, but at least the metal floor was a cold and pleasant contrast with the air temperature. We were settling in when a couple of crewmen started cracking bad jokes, loudly.

"Yeah, we caught a few rounds the other day, nice little bullet holes in the bottom of the plane. You guys be sure to put your luggage up underneath you so you won't get your balls blown off."

They shut the cargo doors, closing out all light except for the little that seeped through small, high portholes. Someone hollered that no one should walk around, as if that were possible in the sardine-can compartment.

After 30 minutes of check-listing at the end of the flight line, the plane took off.

The flight was short, and those who took the bullet-hole remarks to heart could've gotten by without sitting on their gear.

Iron Butterfly

Chapter 9: Moving out

The next five days brought me in contact with solders whose duties were at opposite ends of the mundane-to-murderous spectrum: an ice-cream machine repairman and members of the Iron Butterfly squad.

The former was at Camp Enari, the 4th Infantry headquarters near Pleiku.

Pleiku sat in a valley sprinkled with breast-like hills and flanked by mountains. It was dingy, at least the small part of the city I could see during the bus ride from the air base where the C-123 had landed. The only colorful image I saw through the wire-meshed windows was the white-pillared Vietnamese headquarters of the highland province, also called Pleiku. The edifice stood off the highway, surrounded by cannons and shiny-helmeted guards. It looked like a gaudy Southern mansion and was testimony to the national fascination with colored cloth.

Draped from every balcony, from every part of the roof, were banners striped with the Vietnamese colors of red and mustard yellow.

The Army camp was much less imposing. It was dry and dusty, an oasis-in-reverse bulldozed out of the green countryside.

As our bus headed toward the compound of my outfit—1st Battalion, 8th Infantry Brigade—it was passed by two trucks full of veteran troops, headed in the opposite direction. When they saw the replacements, they started waving and screaming, "Short!" Some of them dropped their pants and mooned us. Nearly all wore their helmets backward, which GI tradition entitled them to do after they had been in-country for six months.

We started the next three days with calisthenics. Then we ate breakfast, which one morning consisted of C-rations—presumably to warn our stomachs of the frontline indelicacies to come. We quickly learned the finer points of bartering for the olive-green cans. Ideally, one could get rid of such undesirables such as ham and lima beans (more commonly called ham and motherfuckers) and acquire something less undesirable, such as spaghetti. A clever bargainer could end up with more than his allotment of coveted pound-cake or fruit.

The days were filled with last-minute training. We shot our way through a quick fire range, a simulated jungle in which cardboard enemy troops would pop up around us. We were taught to spot land mines and were familiarized with North Vietnamese weapons. From the hills that overlooked Pleiku, we learned to recognize the different kinds of artillery that were being fired on a practice range, and clapped as the bombs burst like dirty flowers in the sky a half a mile away.

During breaks, Vietnamese civilians—we called them dinks—swarmed us, trying to sell everything from jewelry and dirty pictures to cold soft drinks and beer. I spent some of my first Vietnam paycheck on a solid brass bracelet. It was supposed to be a friendship bracelet, although I had no desire to befriend the grubby, sly-looking old woman who sold it to me. I bought it mostly to have something non-regulation to wear, a first step in the direction of the "veteran look."

Soldiers paid the local peddlers with piasters, Vietnam's currency. But when we bought toiletries in the PX or scrounged for black-market liquor behind the EM club, we spent military payment certificates. MPC was meant to keep real U.S. currency out of circulation in Vietnam, where it contributed to rampant inflation. To foil black marketers who would stockpile MPC to buy American goods, the military occasionally changed the color of MPC, rendering it useless to anyone but military personnel, who could legally trade the old color for the new. The certificates that I spent were pink on one side and gray on the other. Decorated with profiles of Miss Liberty, they looked like Monopoly money.

After the three days of training, two dozen of us waited two days for rides to Dak To, the camp from which we'd be sent to our companies. While we waited, we pulled duty.

On the first day, I was assigned to pump gas into trucks. The second day, a buddy and I helped a Spec. 5 who repaired appliances and needed some extra-strong arms and backs to deliver washing machines to the barracks. When we finished with the moving chores, we spent the afternoon handing tools to the repairman as he went about fixing an ice cream machine in the headquarters kitchen. We got free ice cream in return.

The specialist, a slight man, chatted amiably. He told us that he hated to see us go out and fight and maybe get killed. He wouldn't, he said, trade places with us for anything in the world.

I just savored my vanilla cone and speculated that I, for one, would rather get my licks in behind a rifle than behind an ice cream maker.

The Iron Butterfly

That evening, the word came down that a convoy would leave in the morning for Dak To, a village in the Central Highlands area where Vietnam, Laos, and Cambodia come together.

It was still dark when we got up and fell into a line that marched past the office building and supply hut of battalion headquarters. The line halted at the only source of light, the open door of the armory hut. We identified ourselves and went inside to draw weapons, which were rather arbitrarily assigned. Most guys got M-16s.

"We need three M-79 people," said a sergeant who was handing out weapons.

"Anybody here want to carry one of those goddamned things?"

Grenade launchers had more character than rifles; carrying one might prove interesting. I took an M-79 and was pleased to see that it was new.

Others weren't so lucky. There was much whining and cursing when soldiers discovered that the bolts on their rifles were rusted shut. Some managed to get replacements. Other guys were told they'd have to wait until they reached their companies, where they might be able to trade for M-16s in better condition.

After getting ammunition, helmets and flak vests, we picked up our packs and duffel bags and headed out to wait for the trucks. They arrived as the sun was breaking over the mountains. We hopped on after lining the truck beds with soft gear and sandbags as a little insurance against explosions.

The convoy was one of the biggest of the year, with hundreds of trucks moving north on Highway 14. Although the idea had been to leave Pleiku early, giving the enemy as little notice as possible of our presence, it was midmorning before the truck that I was riding began to jockey for position in line.

As we began to roll, I watched the various lightly and heavily armed vehicles that slipped into position every 10 trucks or so. Particularly noticeable among the olive-drab Army trucks were the dark, forest-green armored cars of the South Vietnamese troops. These vehicles, with their six huge wheels and little cannons, zipped in and out of the convoy, their bright banners flapping in the wind.

There were three or four American vehicles painted the same dark, glossy green. They were deuce-and-a-halves, or six-bys, such as the one I was in—two-and-a-half ton, six-wheel-drive trucks with canvas covers and racks in the back for passengers. They were armored and equipped with the firepower and manpower to destroy nearly anything that threatened the movement of troops.

These were killer machines, and the one I saw parked outside Pleiku had a quad-50 machine gun mount, a four-barrel, .50-caliber weapon, the kind that had been used during World War II as anti-aircraft guns. It was raised so it could fire over the truck cab and was enclosed by armor plate. The truck had wheels with silver-painted rims and hubs. Its glossy green paint boasted red trim and pinstriping. Across its backside were the words Iron Butterfly, carefully and colorfully copied from the "In-A-Gadda-Da-Vida" rock album cover.

The six men who lounged inside the Iron Butterfly cab or leaned against the side of the truck wore chrome helmets, striped jungle fatigues and boots with white laces. They looked like hard men as they sat or leaned in silence, smoking cheroots. I watched them in fascination as they got in the truck and drove ahead into the convoy.

Wailing at the river

The convoy proceeded smoothly for an hour and a half. The men in my truck began to dig into the fruit juice, beer, soda and C-rations given to us for the six-hour trip. We took turns hopping out, whenever the trucks stopped for a moment, to heed the call of nature. Once, when another guy and I were standing at the side of the road, our truck took off without warning. We started running. The other fellow jumped into the open back of the truck. I lunged after him. Two guys grabbed me and kept me from falling into the road.

After that, we followed the advice of the old-timers and simply urinated over the back rail whenever the truck stopped. It was a straightforward approach to relieving oneself that the Vietnamese accepted as perfectly natural. It also thinned the ranks of local urchins who ran up to the trucks trying to sell doodads and drinks.

In early afternoon, an explosion and the sound of gunfire from the front brought the trucks to a screeching halt.

"My God, we're being attacked," someone yelled. Our driver leapt out, followed quickly by his passengers. We formed a perimeter at either side of the road and aimed our weapons into the lush countryside.

The Vietnamese armored cars sped past beside the highway, tearing up the ground. The only other sign of trouble was smoke billowing in the direction of the sporadic explosions and firing.

The firing stopped in five minutes. In 20 minutes, word came back that there had been "just a little altercation up in the front. Everybody inside." The convoy inched forward. Before long, the trucks approached a river that had two old stone watchtowers on each side. Three of the towers were toppled, but one on the far side stood in all its French-colonial glory. As my truck drove over the bridge, I could see ramshackle hooches surrounding the intact tower. Down at the riverbank, Vietnamese men and women were dragging civilian-clothed bodies from the brown water. I heard wailing over the rumbling of the convoy.

When we reached Dak To, I heard what had happened.

The bridge was guarded by South Vietnamese, whose families stayed near them in hooches below. With a stroke of poor timing, the guards decided to catch their dinner as the convoy approached. Their first mistake was to go fishing with hand grenades; their second was to do it as the Iron Butterfly was passing by.

When the Iron Butterfly gunners heard the grenades explode, they opened fire and decimated the fishermen and anyone else who got in the way.

From then on, whenever anyone mentioned the killer mentality, I envisioned red trim on dark green paint and silver helmets that glinted in the sun.

Chapter 10: Dak To days

Dak To had been overrun by the North Vietnamese a year earlier, during the 1968 Tet Offensive. There had been serious fighting to retake it.

As a defensive position, Dak To left a lot to be desired. It was in a narrow valley next to a river. Mountains closed in on the bullet-ridden bunkers—which consisted of old reddish-gray sandbags shored up by old reddish-gray ones—and rows of tents and canvas-topped buildings.

What the encampment lacked in defensibility, it apparently made up for in strategic location. It served as a supply and command center for troops fighting in the highlands. It was the base camp for the 1st of the 8th "Bullets," to which I reported.

"Glad to see you, Pvt. Myers," said the sergeant who checked my name off a list, then proceeded to take away my new gear. The new pack, the new web gear, even the new extra clothes I'd been issued at Pleiku would be sent to the front lines—it didn't seem to matter that that was where I was headed. I was allowed to keep only the reasonably clean clothes on my back and my helmet and weapon.

"The guys out in the field need these," the sergeant said as he took my uniform. "We have a company laundry at Pleiku. We send clothes out once every few weeks, whenever we get to it. When the laundry comes in, you can pick through it and find stuff that fits you."

I transferred my personal gear to an old pack that the sergeant gave to me. It had ripped straps that I later spent an afternoon mending. I carried few belongings.

Anything I didn't want to take into the field, such as my khaki uniform, had been stored in one of the thousands of duffel bags stacked in tiers at battalion headquarters.

Two other replacements joined me in the wait for a helicopter ride to Charlie Company. One was Johnson, a pale, serious Southerner who had been drafted just before he finished college. The other, Medford, was also from the South, but was smaller, younger and less articulate than Johnson.

That night, the three of us slept on cots in the company tent. In the morning, we set out to explore Dak To.

It was a busy, noisy place. Helicopters whirred, jeeps and trucks revved and screeched down the red dirt roads. Every once in a while, a howitzer shell would explode into the mountainous countryside.

The howitzers and their laid-back black gunners were stationed outside the PX, where we stopped to buy doughnuts. The PX consisted of two prefabricated buildings—they looked like truck trailers—joined together and lined with shelves full of snacks, toiletries, cigarettes and magazines. It was a far cry from the department store atmosphere of the exchange at Long Binh.

The whole operation at Dak To looked impermanent compared with the entrenched U.S. presence I'd seen elsewhere. The atmosphere was less regimented. Everyone seemed to be doing a job but, like the gunners who read comic books between occasional radioed orders to fire, no one was uptight about it.

As we wandered back toward the tent, we passed the camp's only permanent building. There was a six-foot wooden fence surrounding what a sign on the gate proclaimed to be the Dak To Officers' Club.

Johnson and I were tall enough to peer through the barbed wire that topped the fence. We found ourselves looking past a patio and through glass doors at a posh establishment that would have been a lot less out of place in Saigon. Officers sat at tables and at the gleaming bar, watching television and drinking liquor that was served by a bartender in a white dinner jacket.

When someone slid open the doors, we could hear the sounds of the club. But the clink-and-murmur was quickly drowned out by the roar of a jeep that kicked up dust in the street. Johnson and I, who'd been giving Medford a blow-by-blow description of what we saw, turned away from the fence. We walked away cursing the privileges of rank and our own, less-fortunate lot.

Replacements could wait as long as a week for a ride to their companies. Meanwhile, the Army made sure their time was not spent idly.

I was assigned guard duty outside the ammunition dump that night with two soldiers from Company A. They had been sent to battalion headquarters from their firebase, where they had been bitten by a dog. They were undergoing a series of painful shots for rabies and were in particularly bad moods.

The three of us were dropped off at one of the huge bunkers that ringed the dump. The cellar-like affair rose slightly above the ground, its earth-covered top surrounded by sloping piles of sandbags. There were eye-level slits in the bunker, but no machine guns mounted inside. In order to hear, see or fire at approaching enemy, the guards had to be outside. We were to serve two-hour shifts, with one man standing guard on top while the other two slept inside the bunker.

It was dusk when one of the Alpha Company soldiers went up to pull the first shift. The other one, settling in below, immediately pulled out a fifth of Suntory whiskey. He offered some to me. In my eagerness to be accepted, I took the bottle. We polished off the booze well before the first shift was over.

When the first guard came down into the bunker and his buddy climbed drowsily up to replace him, the inside of the bunker was completely dark. Before long, a match flared and lit up the earthen walls. This guy was lighting a joint. He held one out to me.

"Hey, let's smoke a few numbers here," he said.

"All right."

I'd never smoked marijuana. This was a red-letter night.

I was pleasantly numb by the time I shouldered the M-79 and headed up for my first stint on guard. I sat down, carefully arranging my grenades and other gear beside me. I gazed out at the moonlit sea of bushes and barbed wire that separated the mounds of the ammunition dump from the hillside a few hundred yards away. I leaned back and stared at the canopy of stars. Then I passed out.

When I woke up, I was below, lying in my bunk. Presumably, the other guards carried me there. I fumbled for my watch and, in the gray morning light that was seeping in the bunker's slits, could see that it was broken. I knew how it happened. That watch had been our only way of telling when to change guards, and the joint-puffing guy had talked continually about "buddy-fucking" his friend by turning back the watch hands to fool him into serving a four-hour shift. He broke the hands when he tried to carry out the threat.

The watch had been a gift from my dad, chosen because it had a black face that wouldn't reflect light and draw enemy fire. Now it was worthless. Pissed off, I went outside and tossed it into the barbed wire.

I didn't have much time to gripe because a jeep pulling a trailer full of replacement guards was pulling up. As I jumped into the trailer for the ride back to the company tent, I couldn't find it in myself to pick a fight. I was feeling too fine for that. To my amazement, the debauchery of the night before had not resulted in a hangover. I was awake, clear-headed and even spared of that morning-after, bottom-of-the-birdcage taste in my mouth.

I rejoined Medford and Johnson. We were told to go to the helipad after breakfast and wait for a ride out.

As we walked across the parade field to the cookhouse, we met a cleanup crew. Its members, apparently being disciplined for some wrongdoings, were followed by a bored-looking sergeant whose hat was pulled down over eyes that scoured the earth for trash.

"Pick it up, pick it all up," the sergeant yelled. "I want every goddamn thing that isn't Mother Nature's picked up off this field!"

The three of us from Charlie Company stood aside and watched as one skinny kid in the crew came across a rat that had been flattened in the dirt, run over by a vehicle. The kid recoiled at the sight and was about to walk around the rat when the sergeant barked at him.

"Just pick up the goddamned thing by the tail and throw it in the trash. Move it!"

His face wrinkled with disgust, the soldier picked up the rat, carried it five feet and dropped it in the trash can beside me. Then he turned and went back to get a more interesting piece of litter—a bush hat.

I'd spotted the hat, too, and reached it first. It was a real prize. Bleached by the sun from green to tan, it had a narrower brim than the newer bush hats. It would definitely give its wearer that old-timer look, and I was pleased to find that it fit my big head.

The baseball-style cap I'd been wearing was scorned by many of the infantrymen, who associated it with training. But I had creased its bill and roughed it up to make it look reasonably veteran-ish—enough so that Johnson, who had lost his hat during guard duty the night before, was delighted when I passed it along to him.

After breakfast, we headed for the flat expanse of red dirt that was the helipad.

We leaned our weapons and gear against an open-sided shelter that looked like a ramshackle bus stop. We watched as a couple of helicopters came and went, their cargo areas unloaded, then filled with supplies.

When the second chopper left, one of the soldiers who had been loading supplies ambled over.

"There may not be any chance of you three getting out of here today. We don't have any orders to ship anybody out. Besides," he said, nodding toward the shelter, "those two guys in there get shipped out first."

Medford, Johnson and I turned our heads and peered inside. The "two guys" turned out to be a lanky soldier and his equally thin dog, who were slouched against each other in the corner. The soldier looked the part of a combat veteran. As he sat there, calmly sucking in the smoke from his cigarette, looked totally at peace with himself. His body seemed to flow into the earth. The German shepherd, lying with paws crossed, was equally at ease.

"How long you guys been over here?" Medford asked. The K-9 didn't look up.

"Oh, I've been over here about eight months. Old Rolph here, he's been over here a coupla three years," the soldier said, reaching over to rub Rolph's ears. "Good ol' dog."

The veteran's demeanor favorably impressed me because I tended to classify all infantrymen as chest-thumpers, full of false bravado, or assholes like the guys from Company A with whom I'd just spent the night.

This guy and his dog were headed to Alpha Company, too. I heard later that the veteran lost his legs and Rolph lost his life when they tripped a mine. The dog had been trained to sniff VC out of tunnels, not to locate mines.

The man and dog were still relaxing in the shelter at dusk when the three of us gave up on getting a ride. We reported back to headquarters and, after dinner, were assigned to pull guard together.

Soon after we got to our assigned bunker, a major drove up. He asked what company we were with and how things were going, then said that he needed someone to go with him and stand watch at another bunker. He pointed to Johnson, who climbed into the jeep.

After they left, Medford and I decided to pull three-hour shifts. I went on top first. I arranged my gear around me, just like the night before, and looked out past the barbed wire. But this time, there was a rapid river below, separating the bunker from the hills that rose steeply from the opposite bank. I reasoned that we fresh fish had been given this position because it wasn't likely that Charlie would swim the river to attack my scrawny ass. My first shift passed without incident. Toward the end of the second one, I spotted what looked like a campfire on the hill across the river. I woke Medford. "Look, activity."

We gleefully called it in and asked for instructions.

"Never you mind, we'll take care of it," came the reply. I finished my guard, watching the fire glow like a firefly and hearing the river rush by. Then I woke Medford again and fell into my bunk. The next thing I knew, the sun was creeping up, the earth starting to get color. I could tell by the sun-lit bunker dust that Medford was shaking off me.

"God, you won't believe what happened. You just won't believe what happened. After you went to sleep 'n' all, the major came back, and he had that recoilless rifle on the back of his jeep."

Medford was so excited he hardly stopped to breathe between his staccato sentences. "He and I kept loading and shooting that thing, and we got off 50 rounds at least at that fire. We could hear trees exploding and we kept watching that damn fire through all the smoke until it disintegrated—poof—it went out. And the major kept laughing and firing, just laughing and firing!"

I wiped the sleep and dust from my eyes and shook my head in disbelief. A recoilless rifle was a long open-ended weapon that spewed detonation gasses out the ass end like a jet engine with the shell blasting out the front at the same time—just about the loudest thing you'd hear and live. I couldn't possibly have missed hearing that.

"Sure, sure," I said, convinced that Medford was trying to pull one over on me.

Then I stepped outside. Leftover casings were scattered all around the bunker.

I was spitting angry.

"What a bunch of shit! Why didn't you wake me up?"

Medford's repeated apologies were no comfort whatsoever.

When we caught our helicopter out that day, I was still heartsick. My first action, and I'd slept through it.

Enemy Below

Chapter 11: *Beaucoup dien cai dau*

At Firebase 30, I joined the second squad of Company C's 2nd Platoon, 1st Battalion, 8th Brigade, 4th Infantry Division.

The squad occupied one small section of a large trench that circled the firebase. The bunkers, which rose slightly above the trench, were makeshift shelters to say the least. The bunker that Medford and I inherited was the oldest and most decrepit of the lot. The others had doors made of wood that their occupants had scrounged, and bunks that sat on tiers. Not this place. It was just a layer of wood and a helicopter door piled with sandbags.

As I crouched to peer into this extremely humble abode, Stotka, the gung-ho squad leader, presented me with two candles.

"The last two guys who were in here didn't take very good care of it, Hoss, but you're welcome to it."

I lit a candle and crawled in. There was just enough room inside for me to sit in a slouch. By the flickering light, I could see that Medford had already laid out his own gear on the softest of the three sleeping spots, so I claimed another.

By the time I'd unpacked my few belongings, Medford had returned to the bunker. Stotka took us around and introduced us to the others in the squad. There were fifteen men at most and it didn't take me long to know some of them fairly well.

There was the squad's only black, Laney. He was a former parole officer from Southern California who sported a slight beard and had an affection for marijuana.

There was Longest, another California doper who had a goatee and a thin moustache that tapered into a rattail on either side. He wore love beads.

There was Fisher, an old man of 26 or 27 from the hills of Tennessee. Fisher, for some reason known only to the Army, was given a 67 prefix on his serial number, which meant that he had failed the Army's minimal IQ test. That prefix kept him from advancing up a pay grade beyond E-4. None of us could figure out how he got stuck with it because Fisher was the resident genius. He had a kinship with anything mechanical and was always called upon to fix things. He was a natural woodsman, a Daniel Boone who was point man more often than not, the one who could sniff out Charlie Cong from a kilometer away. Fisher was the perfect 11 Bravo, aka infantryman. He was the only one in the squad with a Purple Heart earned, I learned later, under less than noble circumstances.

Lynch, a blond Georgian, had a cussedness about him. He was the other point man, almost as good a tracker as Fisher. Lynch carried a pump shotgun and wore a bush hat with shotgun shells stuck in its band.

There was Oates. That wasn't his real name, but he reminded me so much of actor Warren Oates that his real name didn't register. Oates was a short guy with a bristly moustache. He wore a blue sweatshirt, a dark blue jacket with red lining, brown stateside hunting boots, and a fisherman's hat with a flowered hatband.

Andy Day, six-feet-two and lanky, was the happiest to see me. He was the M-60 machine gunner and was looking for someone big enough to replace him so he could take a job as the company's radioman.

Newton and Niederfringer, who'd gone through training together, looked like twins. Moustaches. Sandy hair. Smart in a college sort of way. They were constantly finding a different way to do something. While the rest of us ate unadorned C-rations, these guys made an oven out of tin salvaged from destroyed helicopters and, over heating tablets fashioned from claymore mine composition explosive (C-4), baked pizzas made from crackers and spaghetti with meatballs. They'd sit outside their bunker with kerchiefs around their necks, cooking their meals. For awhile, they invited guests to their pizza fests. But everyone gave them such a hard time that I think they stopped extending invitations.

It wasn't their eccentricities that made me wary of Newton and Niederfringer. Nor was it their affection for C-4, which lots of guys found useful. It was the way the others talked about them.

"Don't hang around those two—they're nothin' but trouble," I was told.

"They're boocoo fuckin' dinky dow."

Beaucoup dien cai dau. Crazy in the head. Off the wall.

"Yeah," Stotka said. "One of these days, they're gonna get themselves killed."

Newton and Niederfringer were given the duty of manning the big, mounted .50-caliber machine gun. The .50, a long-range weapon, was the first thing the enemy went after.

Over the next few days, I got to know men from the other squads. There was Martinez, the schoolteacher from the Southwest who would share the hot salsa and chilies that came in his care packages from home. Hano, the Hawaiian surfer, would pass around canned dried squid for everyone to chew on.

Another batch of replacements came in, and one of the strangest of them bunked for a while with me and Medford. Stiletto was the gung-ho type ("gonna kill Charlie Cong" and "my dad was a Marine") who was always taking pictures with a miniature camera. He also carried a stiletto knife that had a brass-knuckles handle.

There was no greater status symbol for an infantryman than a distinctive knife.

Not to feel left out, I got my dad, a former flight engineer, to send me the survival knife that he'd carried when he flew for the Strategic Air Command It was fine, but it wasn't enough to compete with Stotka, who, every time somebody mentioned knives, would say, "Wait a minute, I've got some knives." Then he'd pull a rag from his pack and unroll it to reveal 10 huge knives. They were $40, $50, $60 Buck knives that his relatives had sent to him.

It was Lynch's obsession with getting a knife that led to my first adventure at Firebase 30.

"Let's raid the mess hooch," Lynch said. "I want to get one of those butcher knives. I want a bigger knife to carry out in the field."

The cook hut looked like one of those wooden buy-your-cabbage-here stands with a bug screen in front and a sloped roof. It was there that the troops lined up and the cook dished out food, the best of which was choppered in several times a week in huge bins.

There was no talking Lynch out of the raid. He had to have that knife.

Stiletto and I, who were getting bored, agreed to go along. The cook slept two hooches down from the cook hut, so we had to be quiet. We took off our dogtags and sneaked to the edge of the hut. I was the lookout near the front door. Stiletto waited at the back. Lynch went in. Clang! Bang! Boom! It sounded as if every pot in the place was crashing to the ground. Lynch came running out the front.

"Goddamnit, let's go!"

They hid inside my bunker, where we discovered Lynch had absconded with a canned ham along with the knife. We had to destroy the evidence. When the ham had been devoured, we threw the can out past the barbed wire in front of another squad's area.

We woke the next morning to the cursing and screaming of the cook. He stormed directly to Lynch's place.

"Come outa there, you little bastard! I know you stole that knife!"

At the cook's accusation, there was only one thing for Lynch to say.

"I didn't do it, honest to God I didn't steal your damn knife. Would I do that?"

A scene ensued, ending with the cook's adamant, "I know it's you, you sonofabitch. If I ever catch you..."

After all his trouble, Lynch was forced to throw the knife away that night so he wouldn't get caught with it.

Lynch had his share of heroics along with misadventures. He'd participated in one of the squad's shining moments, the kind they liked to tell to newcomers as we sat around, weapons across our laps, chowing down.

No medal for this

Earlier that year, Lynch had gone with Stotka, Longest and Day on a short-range patrol. Although they were only supposed to be observers, Stotka wanted firepower. So Day carried the M-60. Lynch had his shotgun; the others toted M-16s.

LRRPs or Long-Range Recon Patrols—aka lurps—usually lasted four days. The third night of this one, after they settled into the jungle in enemy territory, they began hearing voices and rustling around them.

Stotka grabbed the radio.

"We've got enemy activity. I think we're gonna need to pull out," he whispered loudly into the receiver. "We need a chopper." They radioed their coordinates and those of a clearing they'd passed earlier in the day. The plan was to hump back to the clearing and guide the helicopter in with a strobe light. As the four moved to the designated area, they could hear Vietnamese voices and movement not 30 feet away. They could hear the chopper. The radio crackled.

"Three-two Charlie, three-two Charlie, cannot see your strobe."

An NVA battalion had moved in around them. They radioed back that they were still heading for the clearing, and would set up the strobe when they got there.

The North Vietnamese heard the American voices. Some rounds went off over their heads and they started running down the trail, the enemy in pursuit. They ran like hell, all the time with the pilot screaming over the radio, "Are you at the clearing? We're coming." He was following the strobe, which Stotka had snapped on. The brilliant directional light flashed up through the trees as they ran.

The rescuers and the LRRP squad reached the clearing simultaneously. As the chopper started to descend, the enemy let loose a barrage. Tracers arched through the air and the four earthbound hearts sank as the chopper went back up. The helicopter crew was duty-bound to pick up those guys, but it wasn't about to land and get riddled full of holes. So the crew kicked out a 200-foot rope ladder that was used for jungle evacuations.

As Longest told the story, nobody lugging an M-60 ever moved as fast as Day did that night, pulling himself up the rungs. Longest was the first to get up the ladder and haul himself in. As he turned to lean over the edge and yell words of support, another barrage opened up and the pilot took off. Day, Lynch and Stotka were left dangling, hanging onto the ladder for dear life as the chopper rose 2,000 feet in the air.[1]

Their spectacular deed was chronicled in the division newspaper. Not that it was anything that would bring them official recognition, there was no medal for "exemplary retreat" — but it made a story they were damned proud of.

I had to admit it was a good one.

Another episode in the squad's history that accounted for its "through-thick-and-thin" attitude was the NVA takeover of the firebase.[2]

It happened during the rainy season, about two months before I arrived.

The firebase was bombarded for three or four days with mortar fire. Neither artillery nor air power was much help. They couldn't blow up Charlie because they couldn't see him. So Charlie kept firing mortar rounds.

It was tough for helicopters to get in with supplies, but somehow they managed to bring in the battalion executive officer. By the time major so-and-so arrived to assess the situation, the wisdom of evacuation was already obvious to the officers in charge.

The men were ordered to destroy all the sandbags, push down bunkers, tear up all material they couldn't take to keep it out of the enemy's hands. The GIs were waiting for the choppers that would take them out when the major told them things had quieted down and that they were going to stay on the firebase for a few more days.

---

[1] Andy Day remembers that he and Steve Stotka were the ones left clinging to the ladder, which they held onto until the helicopter touched down on a small air strip. Brent Longest recalls that there wasn't a lot of enemy fire because "the Vietnamese were running, too. There was no time to fight."

[2] According to Ted Fisher, it was another firebase – Firebase 29 – that was overrun in November of 1968.

The men were starting to bitch and whine when the NVA hit them with all of its mortars. There were no bunkers to hide in; there was nothing to do but dig holes and pray.

As far as the men were concerned, there was only one bright spot in the dismal situation. The asshole major was stuck there, too. No helicopter was able to land to whisk him to the rear.

Any pleasure the second squad, second platoon derived from the major's stranding was obliterated when he chose three of them to build a bunker to house the officers—in the middle of the barrage.

Nobody was hurt during construction, and Fisher and some of the others even managed to build a small bunker for themselves. But Fisher was grazed by shrapnel when his hand was sticking out of the entryway of the bunker, and he was written up for a Purple Heart. The injured hand had been holding a microphone. Fisher had been taping the battle sounds for the folks back home.

When the bombardment ceased that night, it was decided that everyone would get out. Just about the time they'd torn down the bunkers again, the mortaring started up.

Once more, the major insisted that the bunker be rebuilt. This time a round went off and wounded the men who were working on it. The major wrote himself up for a Silver Star for heroism in the face of the enemy. That didn't sit well with the troops.

Finally, the helicopters came. The company moved out, but not without a firefight with the NVA, who were moving in. Second platoon, the last off the hill, caught the brunt of the fighting.

The squad spent the next two months guarding an old stone bridge. It was close enough to a village that some of the local lovelies would pop out occasionally to earn a few extra piasters. The bridge was also close enough to battalion headquarters that the brass was upset by this kind of fraternization.

A jeepload of MPs came by more than once to warn the squad to stay away from the boom-boom girls. Finally, Lynch and some of the others got into a fistfight with the badly outnumbered MPs. The leader of the unwelcome visitors finally picked himself up, screamed, "OK, you bastards, you've had it—you're all going to LBJ," and drove off.

Half an hour later, the jeep returned, followed by two truckloads of MPs. They were armed to the teeth and hot to make some arrests. Faced with the possibility of stints in Long Binh Jail, Fisher and Lynch climbed to the guard post and got behind the platoon's .50. They fired 20 rounds above and in front of the jeep. The police put their vehicles in reverse and disappeared.

The next day, the battalion commander came out. He told the squad that, because of the entire company's behavior, they were being moved back to Firebase 30.

They were told it had been retaken, although the men decided that the NVA had simply chosen to walk off that miserable knoll.

Unspoken act of cowardice?

Despite horror stories I'd heard about some of the previous honchos on the firebase, I had no major gripes with the officers I served under. One of the most interesting was my platoon leader, a dashing first lieutenant whose thinness earned him the nickname Stork.

Stork took pride in being an infantry officer. His lean face, with its little moustache, was shaded by an old-style Army Ranger's hat, which meant he had gone through Ranger school, the preliminary step to Green Beret training. It was his first tour in Vietnam.

The military had long been part of Stork's life—his father, a wealthy timber industry executive, was a retired admiral—which might have helped forge his gung-ho approach to combat. But the biggest influence on him was the death of his twin brother, who had gone to Nam early in the war and had been shot.

In a session of swapping life stories with me, Stork made it clear that his reason for joining the Army was to avenge his brother's death. His only interest in life seemed to be killing Cong. What separated him from other kill-crazies was his total disregard for his own safety. He seemed to go out of his way to put himself in the enemy's crosshairs. Others took customary precautions to hide their rank and avoid being seen using the radio for fear of becoming targets. Stork kept his insignia polished and made a show out of using the radio. He wore his Ranger hat and badge everywhere.

Charlie Company's executive officer was a slight, pale, aristocratic-looking lieutenant called Pinky. Pinky struck me as the most ill-fitting of nicknames, because the exec had none of the cutesy, nincompoop traits I associated with the word. Quite the opposite. Pinky seemed the pensive type, inclined to gaze quietly out into the highland mists.

While bold displays of eccentricity were the rule among the combat zone troops, Pinky seemed to turn inward. I didn't understand why Pinky was almost universally disliked, why no one wanted to talk with him. Was his ostracism, like his nickname, rooted in some unspoken act of cowardice? My first encounter with Pinky occurred when the exec showed up at dusk in my bunker doorway. No one was around but me and Medford. Pinky stood there, with a foot propped on one of the bunker's planks, and asked, "How are you guys?" A rather one-sided conversation ensued, with the officer spending the better part of 30 minutes on the subject of bunker rats. He went into great detail about why he despised the rats. It was an unsoldierly lecture, containing not one four-letter word. Then he said, "Have a good night," and walked off.

Pinky seemed to be an outcast, and his greatest torment was a guy in our second platoon. The tormentor—a swarthy 30-year-old with a bushy moustache and perpetual five o'clock shadow, so I thought of him as Shadow—made it his avowed object in life to kill Pinky. He would follow Pinky around, to the point where Pinky was driven to take refuge with the officers on the other side of the hill just to get away from the guy.

When Shadow wasn't on duty, he would sit and sharpen his bayonet outside Pinky's door. When Pinky would write him up for goofing off, Shadow would reply, softly, "I'll kill you for that." Because he was very short when I got to the firebase—

with only a week before his return to The World, Shadow was intensifying his anti-Pinky campaign.

I had no idea what prompted Shadow's vendetta, but I saw it reach a peak of insanity on Christmas Eve. At the time, Pinky was in charge because Capt. DeHart, the company CO, hadn't returned from his Hawaiian R&R.

Christmas madness

I'd been on the hill for a day when the cook decked out the food hut with Yuletide bunting. Choppers flew in with bins of hot holiday meals. Along with the food and mail came tasseled, tissue-lined, gold-lettered menus. Each one was stamped with a red and green shield of the United States Army in Vietnam and an address indicating the forthcoming turkey a la king had made its way to the front lines compliments of Gen. Creighton Abrams, commander of all U.S. forces in South Vietnam.

We sat around a Christmas tree that had been fashioned out of a pile of debris, digging into what turned out to be not turkey, but ham. Along with the ham slices came some undistinguished vegetables, cold mashed potatoes and promising-looking dressing.

I was among the first to delve into the dressing, and the first to notice something wrong with it. Its mushy consistency was marred by hard, sharp chunks. I grabbed my carton of milk, rinsed my mouth and spat out the offending material.

Soon everyone was finding pieces of glass in their dressing. This bit of holiday cheer came compliments of an enemy sympathizer who worked in the kitchen at battalion headquarters. Because the culprit didn't have the common sense to grind the glass finely enough to be less noticeable, no one was hurt. The same could not be said for him. The company heard later that, when the glass had been traced back to him, he'd been shot "trying to escape."

After polishing off the ham, we settled down for some serious refreshments. Bottles of booze started coming out of hidden spots. There was some pill popping, much beer drinking. Marijuana provided a seasonal fragrance.

I wasn't indulging in the pot or booze because I was scheduled to pull my first listening post that night. LP meant going out beyond the barbed wire with another guy and listening for enemy activity. In two-hour shifts, one soldier would sleep in a shallow defensive position while the other sat, heavily armed, on top. It was a dangerous job. To fall asleep while on guard was to take a good chance at never waking again. Naturally, LP was assigned to the freshest fish.

It was getting dark. I, Medford and another newcomer were saddling up for night watch when one of the old-timers stopped us.

"Nah, you don't wanna be going out there. It's Christmas. You fellas pull watch up here. C'mon, you can pull it over on top of my bunker." It didn't take much persuasion to keep us from heading down the trail, though I felt uneasy about copping out on my first real infantry duty. When we reached the designated bunker, I settled in on top with my M-79 and arranged on or about myself all of my regulation gear—flak vest, helmet, grenades, and gas mask. I was particularly proud of the mask. It was fitted with a pair of brass-rimmed prescription glasses, without which I'd definitely miss any action while gassed.

Before long, Charlie Medford disappeared. The celebration was going full blast. Guys were rolling down into the trenches. Guys were yelling: "Jeezus, I sure love this fucking place, this is so outstanding!" Guys were coming out from underneath at regular intervals gasping for breath or vomiting.

Someone intermittently emerged from the bowels of the firebase to offer me a beer. I accepted, telling myself that any semblance of serious guard duty had already been shot to hell.

The madness snowballed. I was getting quite looped and started to hear crackling over the radio. No, not crackling. Cackling. Someone was making chicken sounds over the military channels.

"It's chicken man! Bawk ... Bawk ... Bawwwk! It's chicken man!" crowed the voice. "I'm in the fuckin' Army, you can't come and fuck with me!"

"Is that you, Jackass Joe?" came another voice.

"No, that's me."

"Who're you?"

"I don't know, who are you?"

A third voice; "Those people who are responsible for this activity will report themselves."

First voice: "Fuck you. Bawk...Bawk...Bawwwk!"

As the radio madness continued, two men came staggering out with a handful of silver flares. They pulled the lids. Pow! Whoosh! Pow! Whoosh! Soldiers on the other side of the hill started sending up flares, too. They were whizzing by me from both directions. A sustained ratatatatatata joined the cacophony as some of the drunks further on down the trench rediscovered their machine guns.

A handful of people wearing gas masks ran past me, pulling gas grenades from pouches and tossing them left and right. Soon a thick pall of riot gas was creeping along the ground, seeping into bunkers. As I pulled on my mask, tracers started whizzing by my head. Somebody was on the hill, shooting at me. Deciding that my life was the only thing I might be able to guard at that point—if there were enemy about, I wouldn't have known it, much less been able to do anything about it—I snagged the radio, "chicken man" still blaring, and crawled down into the bunker.

The only other man left inside was lying on his stomach in a top bunk, reading a Sergeant Rock comic book by the light of a candle. He was also wearing a gas mask. Our heavy, filtered breathing was the only sound besides the drunken laughter and occasional explosions from above. I scrunched into a bottom bunk, wishing I hadn't left my beer on top. The riot gas had made it virtually undrinkable, anyway. So I sat more or less soberly watching candlelight flicker through the white haze, waiting for the madness to calm down.

Suddenly, along with the gas that billowed in the doorway, there jumped a frenetic figure, laughing through a gas mask and aiming his M-16 with one arm. Without a pause, the intruder squeezed the rifle's trigger and riddled the opposite bunker wall, chewing holes in some bunks and girly posters, narrowly missing us. I dropped to the floor. The guy who had been reading jumped to his feet and started screaming, "You crazy idiot, you stupid fuckhead," as he hit the offender on the head with his comic book. Unfazed, the figure turned to leave, pausing only long enough to yell, "Hoss, Hoss, you coming with me, come on buddy!"

Crap! I thought. It's the all-American boy.

If that were an order Stotka had given, I chose to ignore it. To go with my drunken fearless leader at that point appeared to be something less than sane, also against my radio-watch orders. I didn't see Stotka the rest of the night.

The gas was getting to me. My skin started to itch. I knew my eyes would soon tear up, my face would swell and nausea would begin. I turned to the other guy, who was once again engrossed in the adventures of Sergeant Rock.

"Hey, I'm supposed to be on LP on top, so I'm leaving."

"That's OK, you go ahead and leave."

I snatched the radio, staggered up and out. The idea of abandoning my post didn't sit well with me, but neither did the idea of getting sick.

I went back to my own bunker and found the entire squad's area deserted. I turned around, found a relatively uncontaminated bunker and spent the rest of the night drinking beer with several other refugees from the gas.

Some time after midnight, Shadow came to recruit some of the beer drinkers.

"C'mon, we're gonna go kill Pinky," he said breathlessly. "C'mon!"

Two guys walked out, got their weapons and took off over the hill with Shadow and a few others in the direction of the command hooch. We heard machine guns rattling, mostly M-16s, and grenades exploding.

Through the bunker doorway, I could see an eerie glow from the red and green flares that greeted Christmas Day. Occasionally, someone would set off a huge white flare that turned the night into smoke-filled day. Guys were still running around, buddy-buddy, with no one where he was supposed to be. I'd never seen anything like it.

One thing was certain. I wasn't having a terribly good time.

After the gas had cleared, I went back to the bunker where I'd started to pull LP. I listened to chicken man, who was back on the air, and watched the fourth platoon area erupt in a wild flurry of activity. There were lights and explosions, firing and screaming.

A group of 10 guys went running, full tilt, past me. Shortly before dawn, the South Vietnamese marines manning a firebase five or six kilometers away set off hundreds of flares at once. I watched them shoot into the air, like the spray from a faraway Fourth of July sparkler, before I dozed off.

Shorter than he thinks

The next morning was bright and clear, except for a haze left by the firing of virtually every flare on the firebase.

A kind of playground battle fatigue pervaded the hill. I walked over a carpet of Budweiser, Schlitz and Hamms cans on my way to return the radio to its proper squad. Then I made my way back to my own squad's area. The men I passed moved with such hungover slowness that they seemed more like toy soldiers with worn-down batteries than the real thing. Combat ready they weren't.

The firebase was more ramshackle than usual. Not a bunker, not a trench, not a uniform, not a weapon in the company appeared unmarred by the mayhem. And the area inhabited by the second squad, second platoon was the worst.

On this particular morning, what was left of it was deserted. I soon discovered why: Its trench was filled with wretched, stinking, fly-attracting feces. Some clowns from the fourth platoon had taken the sawed-off 50 gallon drums from beneath the nearest two-hole shitter—the drums whose contents were burned with fuel oil every other day—and rolled them into the trench.

The deed was done in retribution for the escapades of Stotka and his cronies, who had thrown a grenade in a fourth platoon bunker that night. They had slightly wounded one man—barely a scratch—and destroyed thousands of dollars worth of hard-to-replace equipment, including the platoon's M-60.

A radio operator had almost bought the farm when Shadow and his drunken commandos had gone after Pinky and riddled the command hooch. The executive officer had fled for his life.

Considering Pinky's narrow escape, it might have been with relief that he heard that Christmas Day that a helicopter was being sent for him. He would have to answer at battalion headquarters for Charlie Company's behavior, especially the misuse of communication channels, a la chicken man. But, as it turned out, that helicopter was also taking Shadow, whose DEROS date was at hand.

"Pinky's shorter than he thinks," said Shadow with a gleam in his eyes as he shook hands with everyone that afternoon. He was absolutely gleeful. Someone handed him a beer that was left from the night before. He guzzled it, saddled up his gear and headed down to the helipad.

Among those making the trip to HQ that day was one of the minor casualties from the melee. When the chopper returned with him the next day, he was besieged with questions about Pinky's fate. We savored his answer for weeks.

"Well, Shadow and Pinky sat across the chopper from each other all the way back and glared. Pinky squirmed and Shadow glared.

"When we landed, neither of them moved right away. Then Shadow gathered up his gear and hopped off, starting to walk away. So Pinky got off. Then Shadow turned around, real quick—fuck, you shoulda seen him—and grabbed Pinky by the shirt. And he said, 'Pinky, I'm gonna let ya live.'"

Pinky didn't return to Firebase 30.

The pyrotechnics of Christmas Eve had earned the company the nickname of Combustion Charlie, but not everyone was amused. The battalion commander ordered the men to straighten up and fly right. The platoon sergeant, who looked like a fat Glen Campbell, ordered us soldiers to police our areas. It took them two days just to pick up the spent, silver flare casings. As a new fish, I was gratified to be ordered to pull extra daytime at a perimeter OP, observation post, thereby avoiding the detail that involved ridding the squad's trench of shit.

The week's re-disciplinary efforts included a visit from two Vietnamese barbers who were flown out to give haircuts to our motley crew. The clippings were followed by a real treat—a technique the barbers had of grabbing a man's head and giving it an unexpected, sharp yank to the side. The neck-popping maneuver released all tension from the body and was much appreciated by the soldiers, some of whom were just then fully recuperating from the holiday revelry.

Charlie Company was looking less like a bunch of lunatics and more like a combat infantry outfit by the time Capt. DeHart returned from R&R.

DeHart was a Grecian-nosed, professional-looking man. He had only a few months left in Vietnam and liked to talk about how he was going back to Denver to finish school. He was less flamboyant than the grunts under his command—his only non-regulation mark was the small bleeding heart painted on his helmet—but, when he came around to shake hands with the new men, he struck me as the kind of CO who would tolerate the eccentricities of men who were otherwise good soldiers.

Crawford, second platoon's machine gunner, finally got his lobbied-for assignment as the platoon leader's RTO. Although they could understand his enthusiasm, the others in the squad voiced disgust at how quickly Crawford, after six months on the team, cleared out his bunker and moved to the platoon leader's hooch. He didn't stop to give so much as a nice-knowin'-ya slap on the back. It was as though he couldn't wait to start kissing brass.

Mad minute

True to Stotka's word, I inherited the M-60. They gave my M-79 to Stiletto.

With the possible exceptions of the officers and radiomen, the M-60 machine gunner was the most visible and noisiest target in combat. Because he couldn't lie down to provide covering fire in the jungle, because he was burdened with the heaviest, bulkiest weapon and because he had the firepower of a one-man army, he was the sniper's favorite target. From my point of view, carrying the M-60 was tantamount to a death sentence. The afternoon I got the new assignment, I was pissed. Hell, first I hadn't wanted to be in the infantry, then I hadn't wanted to be in the 4th Infantry. Now this.

Then a sense of fatalism set in. I figured I was going to get shot anyway, so I might as well do what I was told. If I was going to be a machine gunner, I was going to be a damn good one.

I took some consolation from the fact my M-60 was probably the best in the battalion. It was new, an M-60E1, which had a higher cyclic rate of fire than the old M-60A1. It had been with the company for only a month and came with a cleaning kit. It even had an extra barrel, which could come in handy in the field because a barrel could begin to melt after several minutes of continual firing. In combat, the man with the M-60 kept 20 rounds of ammunition in a belt in the gun and wore 300 rounds looped across his chest. An assistant machine gunner behind him carried additional rounds.

With the Christmas demise of the fourth platoon's M-60, the only other one in the company besides second platoon's belonged to the first platoon. It was assigned to Johnson, my tall friend from Dak To. It was also an E1, but was in less than prime condition. So the company looked upon me and my gun as its first line of defense.

After a refresher lesson in the care and feeding of an M-60, I sat down on top of my bunker to get to know my weapon. I pulled out my small ringbinder pad from AIT, with its scrawled notes on the "M-60 machine gun ... 43 inches long, 23 pounds unloaded, tripod weight 42 pounds"—thank God I didn't have to carry one of those—"basic load, 600-900 rounds; maximum range, 3,725 meters; tracer burnout, 900 meters; belt-fed, fires 7.62 rounds."

I ran my hand over the black plastic forepiece and butt stock. I flipped up the sight and the carrying handle, flipped down the bipod legs. Then I stripped the gun down, laying about 15 parts on a white towel. From an olive drab plastic bottle that became a permanent fixture in my helmet band, I squeezed the oil that kept the gun functioning despite the ravages of dirt and humidity. The fluid looked like semen. In what became a daily ritual, I rubbed it on and wiped it off the metal, remembering with a grin how one trainee dumbfounded an officer by knowing what LSA stood for ("Lube oil, semi-fluid, grade A, sir!").

When I'd reassembled the M-60, Stork, Stotka and some of the others decided to test the mettle of their new machine gunner. After issuing the standard alert that the upcoming fire was friendly, they ensconced me on a bunker and directed me toward what served as the base firing range. I took aim at a tenacious limb that jutted from a gnarled, bullet-ridden tree 100 yards away. It had been the target of countless free-fire sessions. I proceeded to shoot it in half. My audience reacted with back-slapping glee.

"Out-fuckin'-standing!"

"Way ta go, Hoss!"

"Hey, you're pretty good."

I was pretty good with weapons, which was a source of pride to them all, especially Stotka. They liked to watch me in action during the daily mad minute. That was a free-fire period that served as a means of testing weapons and reminding the enemy of the American presence. The CO alerted the squad leaders of the exact time to start shooting, and they in turn passed the word to the troops. Every soldier dropped what he was doing, gathered his weapons and walked to the perimeter.

Mad minute could be called at any time, but seemed to come most often at dusk.

I suspected that the officers liked to watch the tracers shoot through the settling darkness. From my position, I could feel the setting sun on my back and watch the hill's shadow fall on the orange-tinged mountains to the east. The animals below, clued to the coming barrage by the hubbub at the perimeter, chattered, squawked and—to the chagrin of us target-seeking marksmen—disappeared into the jungle.

From the M-60 came bursts of eight rounds at a time, ta-ta-ta-tau ta-ta-ta-tau.

The M-16s made loud, high pitched brrrrrrraaaatttts. Grenades shot from the M-79s with a phoont!, followed by a pause and then a crump! as the fist-sized ammo hit. One squad leader fired a captured AK47 on semi-automatic, making a constant clack-clack-clack.

From the shotgunners came a rhythmic shuck-shuck-boom! shuck-shuck-boom! as they pumped and fired.

An unheard whistle, waving of hands and the men's practiced sense of timing told them when the 60 seconds were over.

When I wasn't firing the M-60, I usually had an M-79 in my hands. I knew how to judge the thrust and angle of the arcing grenades and liked the challenge of making them fall exactly where I'd planned. Sometimes I'd fire the .45 I was given along with the machine gun. The pistol was in good shape. Although it had been in the company for a long time, its barrel was new—thanks to Lynch and Crawford, who had acquired it by sneaking into Pinky's hooch and swapping the original barrel with one from the exec's mint-condition .45.

We called the enemy Charlie. The term came from the phonetic spelling of Viet Cong—Victor Charlie, or VC, the North Vietnamese guerilla fighters. But we always called enemy fighters Charlie, even those in the North Vietnamese Army. NVA soldiers which were the first "Charlie" I saw.

I'd spent an afternoon working with Fisher, the squad mechanic, trying to fix the .50-caliber machine gun that sat on the second platoon's side of the hill. Newton and Niederfringer hadn't kept it clean and, eventually, the bolt release and the bolt latch release lock on the buffer tube sleeve went awry.

When the .50-caliber seemed to be functioning again, thanks to a scrounged replacement part, Fisher and I mounted the heavy-assed gun and tripod back on its bunker with sandbags in front of it. As Fisher tested it by firing at a number of distant trees, he and I followed the graceful arcs of tracers that fell to the green valley below.

After breakfast the next morning, as I was sitting on top my bunker reading, someone came running through, yelling "C'mon, c'mon, we've got some activity out there, real enemy!" Like kids behind an olive drab Pied Piper, we ran after him. He stopped behind the .50.

Fisher was behind the machine gun. The growing audience around the bunker, some of them sipping final cups of coffee, gazed at the lush landscape. At this time of day, the valley was a mist-filled, inland Bali Hai. Waves of mountains rose and fell around it. Nearly two klicks away—we estimated distance in kilometers—were several specks that were Montagnard huts, near the line where fields of tall grass on the valley floor met the jungle. Between the huts and the general direction of the firebase, a trail meandered along the edge of dense vegetation.

On the trail, scampering like mice in the direction of the base, were two North Vietnamese soldiers. Those of us with binoculars could see the tan uniforms and gray packs of the enemy. Not enough to justify artillery, but plenty for the .50 cal.

By the time Fisher had the big gun loaded, all of the officers had come down to watch the action. The peanut gallery was getting noisy. I felt privileged to have had a front row seat on top of the bunker.

"Shut up, shut up," someone yelled. "Let Fisher do it. Fisher'll take care of 'em!"

Fisher locked the gun back. "I think they're about in range," he said.

He pressed the butterfly trigger. Ta-ta-ta-toom! Ta-ta-ta-toom! Thirty pairs of eyes followed the tracers that flew into the valley and kicked up dust along the trail.

"Shit," Fisher said as his prey skipped into the jungle.

"Shit," echoed the Pied Piper. "All we did was scare 'em a little bit."

"Yeah," another grunt replied in disgust. "Well, I'm betting they filled their drawers, anyways."

Like kids leaving a movie in which the bad guys got away, they left in quiet groups. They crumpled their coffee cups, slung their binoculars over their shoulders and walked away. I jumped down and waited for Fisher.

Fisher scanned the trail for a few more moments. He cursed, flicked the machine gun top tray open and kicked the empty belt links off the bunker. Then he left, too.

Footsteps in the jungle

That first week on the firebase fulfilled my prime requirement for a happy life: It was interesting. Although the hill was secure, we carried weapons with us at all times.

And when I went out to pull OP, the fact that I was in enemy territory heightened my senses and kept my adrenaline flowing. When I was in the relative safety of the barbed wire, I could sit and write letters or swap stories with the other guys. I was almost one of the team now.

On New Year's Eve, Stotka announced that he, I, Longest and Medford were going on a slurp.

There would be no need for the heavy M-60 on this reconnaissance patrol, so I borrowed Laney's M-16. Laney handed the rifle over with the admonition that "you'd best not fuck it up or I'll take you out with what's left of it." Then he helped me suit up, telling me what provisions to take for a few days in the bush.

With bush hats on our heads, packs on our backs and rifles held at ready, our quartet passed through the perimeter, passed the OP people, cleared our mission on the radio and headed down the trail. Stotka led us, compass and map sticking from his shirt pocket.

I was excited. This was soldiering.

The width of the trail varied, but for the most part it dictated that we walk single file. We moved steadily, but not quickly. We weren't afraid of mines because we knew

Charlie used the same trails and wasn't likely to risk blowing himself up. Because we knew the enemy could be in any tree, around any turn, our eyes kept moving faster than our feet, surveying the dense foliage that grazed our elbows and filtered the sunlight.

Half a kilometer from the firebase, we struck off the main trail and came upon the remains of an enemy staging area. There were four abandoned hooches, each tent-shaped, bamboo and rush-matted with a small cooking area in front. Judging by the leaves that were covering everything, we surmised that the camp had not been used for several weeks. I found pamphlets directed at the North Vietnamese, urging them to surrender to their friends in the south. The propaganda had apparently been destined for use as kindling.

I stuffed a few of the pamphlets in my fatigue pocket for souvenirs.

We kept moving. It was steamy, but the jungle canopy and our relatively light packs made the heat bearable.

By late afternoon we were looking for a place to camp. We found one at the top of a ridge, 25 or 30 feet off a trail. We threw down our packs and broke out the canteens.

"Hell, we're going to need some water pretty quick," Longest said after glugging down half his supply. Stotka nodded. He consulted his maps and turned to me and Medford. "You jokers head down the hill and see if you can find some water. I think there's a stream down there, at least it says so on the map."

We grabbed rifles and canteens and started bushwhacking down the steep incline. A tangle of vegetation tugged at our boots. We climbed over trees that grew at odd angles in their search for sunlight. For 45 minutes, we slapped at mosquitoes and sweated until we dripped, only to find a dry streambed. We drained our canteens before starting back up the hill.

Stotka seemed unsurprised that we hadn't found water. It was almost as if he hadn't expected the new guys to fulfill such a mission. He and Longest, the veterans, would have to take over the search.

"All right, you guys, sit here and watch the radio," Stotka told us. "We're gonna head west for the river at the foot of this hill."

As I watched them head toward the trail, I turned down the squelch on the radio as far as it would go. I didn't want any incoming calls to wake every bird around. Then Medford and I arranged our gear around us and lay down on our poncho liners, facing in opposite directions. I pulled out a letter to my folks that I'd started writing at the firebase.

I'd only written a few sentences when I heard footsteps coming through the forest. I grabbed my rifle and spun in the direction of the crump, crump, crump. What the hell was this, the Cong coming up hill through the trees? Medford read the unspoken question in the confusion on my face.

"It can't be them," he whispered. "They'd be coming down the trail."

Should we call for help on the radio? We decided against it. Help was too far away. Besides, calling would make too much noise. There was nothing to do but aim our locked and loaded M-16s and hold our breath.

The footsteps and sound of trees being brushed aside stopped at what couldn't have been more than 15 feet away. But the foliage was so dense that we still couldn't see anyone. Our stomachs were lodged in our throats.

The intruder began moving again. Suddenly, he thrust his head through the edge of the thicket not six feet from us. It was the big, ugly, bearded head of a huge orangutan. Below the head, where two hairy hands had parted the brush, was the brightest orange critter I'd ever seen.

The orangutan peered at us, lifting his drooping eyelids momentarily then lowering them in apparent indifference. He dropped his hands, closing the jungle curtain that exposed him, and sauntered off.

"My God!" I wheezed with a mixture of relief and glee. We chuckled for 10 minutes. It was an old joke: a gorilla, not a guerilla.

Soon the radio crackled softly.

"We have a report of NVA in your area, a party of 20 drawing water along the river west your position. Copy?" an RTO at the firebase said.

"Roger! Two of our guys are down there now. Will keep you advised," I answered. There was nothing they or we could do but wait. I finished my letter.

Before long, Stotka and Medford returned, sloshing canteens on their belts and mission-accomplished grins on their faces. When I told them about the radio report, Stotka looked up the coordinates I'd been given. The enemy had been getting water just around the bend in the river from where he and Longest had been.

We didn't dare start a cooking fire. A patrol as small as ours couldn't risk a run-in with an entire NVA unit. So we ate canned peaches and spent a sleepless night expecting to be shot at. But the jungle was calm. In the morning, we moved out. We stayed off trails, instead moving down the side of the hill. The prickly brush hit our faces, pulling skin off our cheeks. It scratched our hands, tore holes in our uniforms and hung onto our packs. Sweaty and sticky with bugs, we were pleased to come out of the dense brush and find a stream where we could wash up.

The swift water was overhung with trees, and we decided that its banks would be a reasonably safe place to spend the night. We built a small fire, heated water in a metal canteen cup and poured it into LRRP ration bags.

Lurp rations were a luxury. They were man-sized meals—in this case, chili and spaghetti—that had been freeze-dried and put in plastic bags. They were much lighter than C-rations, which made them ideal for carrying on long missions. They were also tastier than C-rations which meant they were often in short supply for bush grunts because rear-echelon gourmands would pocket the meals that were due to be shipped to combat zones. A package designed to hold 20 packets often was down to four by the time it reached a firebase.

Helicopter crews reported more enemy activity in the area, and the next morning our patrol was summoned back to the firebase. We beat feet back over the two ridges we'd crossed and were nearing the base perimeter within half a day.

Stotka stopped us before we reached the top of the hill. The guys pulling OP were probably trigger happy, what with all the NVA sightings, and he wanted to make radio contact with them before the patrol got within firing range.

"Pop smoke and spot your color, over," the guards challenged.

"Roger, poppin' red. Longest reached into the munitions bag for a smoke grenade. He grabbed several before getting the right color.

"For God's sake, don't pop a green one," Stotka grumbled. Crimson smoke wafted into the air, the come-ahead signal was issued over the radio and our tired quartet trooped past the guards and barbed wire. Stotka reported in at the command hooch. Medford and I headed for our bunker. Be it ever so humble, it seemed to us at the moment a great place to crash.

We were approaching our doorway that had a strange blanket nailed over it when Laney came running after us.

"Don't go in there," he panted. "Stay outta there."

"What is this?" Medford asked.

"I got my snake in there."

"Your what?" I demanded.

"My snake, that's what. Let him in my place the first two days you were gone, now he's in your place. He's eatin' all the rats and gettin' rid of 'em. You guys can bunk with us tonight."

I walked over to the bunker, squatted and looked in. Sure enough, there was a green snake in the corner, curled near my air mattress.

Having neither the inclination nor the energy to argue, we crowded in with three other guys that night.

The sun was still a half-opened eye the next morning when Stotka decided the – bunker had to be liberated from its reptilian inhabitant.

"C'mon, Hoss, let's get that snake. I'd like to make some headbands out of him."

Stotka borrowed Lynch's shotgun and I drew my .45. We crept to the bunker and peered in. When our eyes had adjusted to the darkness, we could see the snake, still curled in the corner.

"You gonna go in there and get him, Steve?"

"No, Hoss. Are you?"

"No."

"I know. We'll throw in a smoke grenade. That'll get him out."

Stotka popped the pin on the grenade, threw it in and backed off. Poof! Dense, purple smoke poured from the doorway and seeped through the bunker's many cracks. Out of the purple cloud zipped the brilliant, sparkly emerald snake. He was 15 feet long if he was an inch. Nah. Closer to 20 feet.

The snake slithered past the barbed wire into the minefield. I shot after him three times with my pistol. Stotka fired the shotgun and missed, too.

"Hey, brother, I'm not going to be dancing around out in the fuckin' minefield for a lousy snake," I said. The words weren't out of my mouth before Stotka was maneuvering near the barbed wire, trying to get another shot. But the snake slithered into the bamboo and disappeared.

Stotka looked dejected. No headband trophy.

"Get the old bastard"

There was much discussion that day about the latest enemy activity below. By evening, the word came down from Capt. DeHart that the entire company would move out in the morning on a cordon-and-search mission to a village about two kilometers away.

We saddled up while it was still dark. Fourth platoon would start out first, but eventually second platoon would move to the front.

We went down the same trail my LLRP patrol had traveled. It seemed much narrower to me now. I was toting the M-60. I was a big man with a big gun on a path made by small men. The belts of ammo slung across my chest got heavier as the sun got higher. So did my helmet.

The M-60 kept getting caught in the jungle growth. But more aggravating was my pistol problem.

The .45 had come to me with a cheap buffalo hide holster, the kind made and sold all over South Vietnam. The holster was designed to carry another type of auto-pistol and had been altered to accommodate the old .45. It had a snap-latch that supposedly held the weapon in place. But with a round chambered and the well-worn weapon on safety, its exposed hammer would snag and cock back; a gentle bump, and bang! Shot in the leg, or worse. When I heard a click-clack-click and a tug on the holster belt I'd have to stop, take the pistol s-l-o-w-l-y from the holster, hold it out awkwardly squeezing the strap safety, gently pressing the trigger and releasing the hammer all the while wrestling with the M-60. Son of a bitch! About the fourth time I'd done that, I stopped carrying a live round in the chamber. The strong possibility of getting shot in the foot with my own weapon wasn't worth the convenience of having a loaded pistol handy.

The hassles with my weapons slowed me to the point that I lost sight of the man in front of me. I ended up taking a wrong turn when the trail forked. When I realized what had happened, my own disgust and that of the guys behind me who had to backtrack through the heat made the sweaty day that much more aggravating.

On this second trip, I took more notice of the litter along the sides of the trail. It was obvious that this was a byway for more than one army. There were discarded C-ration boxes and cans, burnt flares, smoke canisters, candy wrappers, cigarette stubs, North Vietnamese literature, American literature, shards of glass and spent Chinese ammo casings scattered on either side ... I almost expected to have to step aside for one of those tan-garbed NVA and say "S'cuze me."

There were occasional firing positions dug in along the side of the trail. While everyone else sat down to take 10, Stotka began nosing around one of the firing positions. He jumped into the five-feet-deep covered hole. A few seconds later, he yelped and jumped out. The foxhole had been peppered with a chemical, the powdered form of the irritant in riot gas. It would render the ground uninhabitable for hundreds of years. Brief contact caused itching and nausea.

Stotka was coughing badly. He couldn't seem to catch his breath until the bespectacled medic used canteen water to wash the places where the chemical had touched his skin. He was still wheezing when the squad moved up to take point.

Everyone told Stotka that's what he got for being a goddamned gung-ho jackass.

One hundred and ten men, including a platoon of engineers, were on the mission. So was an obnoxious yellow dog. It was the mascot of the third platoon, which was under strict orders to "keep the damn mutt tied up" during the operation.

The dog yapped and the troops talked as my squad passed to the front. But once we took point, all was quiet. At midmorning, we emerged from the trees and looked down at the village. Between it and us was an oxcart-wide trail that joined the one we were on. Within minutes, we were making our way down the larger trail toward the little village, roughly half of the men on each side. Lynch and Fisher were out front, moving like a couple of Indians. They would dash forward a little and squat, then wave the rest of us forward.

The action was amazingly quiet and synchronized. Just like in the movies.

The quiet was shattered by barking. The third platoon's mutt was charging hell-bent-for-leather down the trail. Louder and louder shouts of "git your gawddamn dawg!" began to echo through the hills.

Everything fell apart.

"You assholes, keep quiet!" hollered back the point men. "You're gonna get us all fuckin killed." The dog chomped into Lynch's pants and began tugging. Lynch kicked at the mutt, lost his balance and fell over in the trail. Capt. DeHart was disgusted by the racket and the lack of discipline. Any element of surprise had evaporated. He ordered two of the platoons to circle the village.

One of the top sergeants pointed to a low, grassy bump and told me to set up the M-60 there and cover the village. From that vantage point, I could see most of the 20-some huts. There were no signs of life among them.

As I squatted to look down the barrel of the machine gun, the seat of my pants split.

I silently cursed the laundry delivery, which so rarely contained trousers big enough for me. My flustered train of thought was derailed by the company RTO, who was standing over my shoulder.

"There's somebody down at the main house there. Look."

A figure moved in the doorway of one of the bigger huts, in the shadow cast by a small portico.

"Get him, dust him up" said someone in the small crowd of infantrymen and headquarters observers that had gathered behind me.

The figure moved into the sunlight. It was an old man with a large bundle of sticks hefted on his bent-over back.

I flinched. We'd all heard stories about the papa-sans and the toddlers who hid explosives in their packages and playthings.

"Shoot that old sumvabitch," someone said.

I looked at the pathetic figure in my gun sight.

"I can't shoot him." I turned to Stork. The lieutenant looked at me, looked at the old man, then looked away from both of us. He gave no order to fire.

"Get him, it's your goddamn fuckin' job," came another voice behind me. "He could be VC."

"Well, we won't know until we get down there, will we?" I asked.

"Shut up and move in," Stork ordered.

We picked up our gear and headed into the village, me with the M-60 at my hip, trained on the old man.

Two *Hoi Chanh*—Viet Cong defectors—were serving as guides for the mission. They approached the man, one from each side, and shoved him to the ground. The sticks scattered everywhere. Although there were some indications that there had been NVA or VC troops in the village at one time, there was nothing on the guy to incriminate him. When the interrogators determined that he was not only innocent, but also blind, they helped him gather his sticks. They decided that he had been left behind because he wasn't able to join the rest of the villagers at their work in the fields.

We halted to rehydrate and eat in the village. Some guys gave the sightless man gifts of sunglasses, candy and cigarettes. He grinned toothlessly and bowed repeatedly toward soldiers who had been rooting for his extinction moments before.

The whole scene was rather anti-climatic. We'd been hyped for action. We hadn't burned any hooches, hadn't rousted a hidden enemy battalion, or fired our weapons. The only chasing anybody did was stumbling after some chickens in a dusty village field, and even those targets managed to elude us. We spent 90 minutes in the village before moving out.

The company spent the afternoon hiking to the opposite side of Hill 29, where the locals were working in the fields. When we took a break, I was among those who headed for the shade of a bamboo-and-grass shed on the edge of a harvested field.

The quiet was interrupted by an argument between Capt. DeHart and the weapons platoon commander, whose men were getting tired of lugging their mortars and ammo around the countryside for no apparent reason. The weapons officer wanted to distribute the load among the infantrymen. DeHart said that was a bunch of shit. The two commanders were a good 50 feet from where I sat, but I could make out most of what they were saying. What I couldn't hear was amply communicated by the pushing and shoving going on. I'd never seen officers go after each other like that.

The commanders stopped short of a fistfight and stomped away from each other.

Before long, the troops heard a helicopter. Someone popped a green smoke grenade, the chopper landed and the mortar dudes threw their equipment into its belly.

They'd evidently talked the captain into having their heavy weapons flown back up the hill.

My squad was in the middle of the march that took off toward the firebase. On the way, we passed a Montagnard village. It was quiet, except for a strange confrontation between a terrified woman and a poodle-sized dog. The dog was at the end of a 10-foot leash, straining toward the woman. She, a typically ageless Asian villager dressed in a typical villager's skirt, was screaming and beating the dog with a 10-foot pole.

They were gnashing at each other when our column entered the village and when it departed.

As we started to climb the firebase hill, the razzing that I'd been taking for the split seam in my pants increased. The incline put my rear about eye level with the top sergeant behind me, and because I wore no underwear—in that sticky climate, none of us did—the hoots kept coming. "Gee, Hoss, honey, I cain't wait 'til we get back!"

The guys were laying on the abuse, but their teasing wasn't as bad as the 100-degree heat and exertion. I was panting. Pretty soon I could concentrate on nothing but putting one foot in front of the other. The sky was glaring and cloudless, but everything around me was going dark.

Halfway up the hill, I felt as if I would fall backward.

The sergeant two steps behind propped me up and then lowered me to the ground. If I'd fallen on the steep trail, I'd have taken out 30 men as if they were a row of dominoes.

I was shaky and clammy, able to see nothing but pair after pair of boots and dusty fatigues passing by.

"Get the medic," the sergeant yelled. "I think we've got a heat case."

The medic ran to where I was sitting, got down on one knee and reached for my pallid wrist.

"My God," the medic muttered. "Hey, Sarge, maybe you ought to let some of the others carry this guy's gear. His pulse is 210."

I protested mildly that I was all right, but could barely find the energy to stand up. Three men distributed my gear among themselves. Another gave me an empty M-16 to use as a crutch.

I dragged myself up what seemed like a 19-mile stretch to the top. I fell back to the end of the column, but finally made it to the perimeter, where a guard helped me through the barbed wire. I collapsed on top of my bunker.

I woke up four hours later, still weak and groggy but in significantly better shape. The old timers in the squad told me to stay off my feet. Someone gave me a beer. The platoon sergeant came by to tell me not to feel bad about feeling bad. Once, the sergeant said, he'd passed out from heat exhaustion, had to be evac'd and spent three days in the hospital.

The beer and exhaustion put me to sleep. The medic came by twice during the night to check on me, but there were no more problems.

Life on Hill 29 became monotonous. I pulled the same guard duty, tested the same weapons, ate the same meals and slapped at the same insects each day.

The post-Christmas discipline had left its mark, so destructive antics were kept at a minimum. For a while the most exciting event was the arrival of the cellophane S-P packs that came with our C-rations. They contained smokes and candies that tasted like civilization.

My favorite packages contained Nestle's Tropical chocolate bars and cigars. While almost everyone fought over the cigarettes, I—along with Stork and a few others—coveted the stogies.

There were two visits from the barbers and one from the doughnut dollies. There was much more excitement over the latter. The Red Cross girls dispensed their goodies in the huge bunker that served as the firebase theater. There was such a crowd in there that the most I got to see of a dolly was one female torso in olive drab.

After two routine weeks, Stork organized a platoon-sized, short-range patrol along the river, south of the firebase.

The next morning, the 30 or so men made what was a fairly easy march to the river. We were traveling light. I was delighted to do without the 10 pounds of helmet that had helped make the last march miserable. I wore my bush hat and carried the machine gun and several days' rations. The unit moved on a trail for a while, then headed down a steep slope. We groped our way through brambles and bushes, sliding and slapping bugs for several hours.

Our trail intersected a stream of brackish green water. We forded the lazy current, then walked in the water along the opposite bank. About the time we were getting fed up with the wading and the godawful greenish-gray leeches that latched onto our skin, the river changed character. The current quickened as a series of rocks created miniature rapids. The water seemed to clear as it swirled into deep pools. We looked at each other as if we'd just found a secret playground. We skirted the rapids, then leaped rock to rock across the river, barely waiting for the order to set up camp.

We took off our shirts and used cigarettes to burn leeches off each other's sweaty hides. Stork sent someone to the top of the hill, where radio contact could be established to inform the firebase of the platoon's location.

Like kids at a swimming hole, we stripped to the buff and took turns playing in the river. Before my turn to splash, I sat on a rock in midstream and served as a guard. I held a borrowed M-16 and was naked except for a bandolier of ammunition around my chest. The sunshine, so oppressive before, felt soothing.

My eyes darted up and down the river and its banks, stopping at bright splotches of flowers that interrupted the thousand shades of green in the landscape. For the first time, I was immersed in the lush beauty of Vietnam. Also for the first time, I noticed the change that had come over my body. It was, except for my reddened face and forearms, its usual bed-sheet white.

But it wasn't fat.

Not fat at all. I had no belly. I grinned. God, I thought, I'd hate to get shot and killed when I'm at my healthiest.

I didn't come close to getting shot during those three days in the bush.

It was particularly fortunate for Stork that we made no contact with the NVA, although he wouldn't have looked at it that way. He persisted in wearing his Ranger hat with its shiny bar and jump wings—a practice the rest of us found almost perverse. He was advertising himself as a primo target for snipers.

Take care of the major

I liked Lt. Stork but was unsure what made him tick. My curiosity was particularly piqued one night when Stork paid me an unexpected visit as I sat on Lynch's bunker pulling my two hours of perimeter guard.

Until he showed up, I'd heard little but the pop, crunch and crackle that always came from the 25-foot-deep sea of bamboo surrounding the firebase. In the stillness, guards could actually hear the bamboo growing. The sound, akin to that of someone walking on twigs, always bothered newcomers, who were sure the enemy was creeping up. I was learning to ignore it.

At 04:00, the radio crackled.

"Three-two Echo, three-two Echo, sitreps, over."

I broke squelch, pressing the radio's receiver button three times as a situation report indicating that all was well. Then I looked up to see Stork, who stood there holding two cans of beer. He handed one to me and sat down.

We drank in silence, hearing only the popping of the bamboo. Suddenly, Stork yelled, "Goddamn it, I can't listen to that shit anymore!" He reached down, picked up two grenades, pulled their pins and threw them out in front of the bunker.

"Get down!" Stork said as he grabbed my head and pulled me to the ground.

Whaam! Whaam! There were two seconds of silence before a voice came over the radio.

"Three-two Echo, three-two Echo, this is three-two. What the hell's going on out there? C'mon, three-two, answer!"

I looked at Stork, then at the radio. I lifted the receiver.

"Uh, nothing, we just, I just thought I had ... "

Stork was taking off.

"Don't tell anybody I was here," he ordered in a whisper.

"Say again, three-two Echo. What's going on?"

"I, uh, I thought I heard somebody out there and I thought it was better to throw grenades than not to," I stammered.

"Don't be doing that sierra without clearance, you understand?"

"Yes, sir!"

"Report to me in the morning."

"Yes, sir, I will."

By the time I showed up at the command hooch five hours later, Stork had already told the commanding officer what had happened. The XO, without mentioning the incident, just told me to turn around and get out.

It wasn't long before the lieutenant was pulled off Firebase 30 and sent to Dak To, where he'd be a training officer. Rumor—our main source of information—had it that the Army, aware of Stork's tendency to flaunt his rank in sight of the enemy, decided the brave young officer wouldn't last much longer on the line. If he was going to be around to be useful to the brass, they'd have to get him out of the line of fire. The men also assumed that his position as sole surviving son might have influenced the transfer.

Before Stork left, he led an ambush immediately downhill outside the perimeter—a nighttime trailside reception for the enemy, who was expected to strike the base yet again.

Battalion headquarters sent a major and a lieutenant colonel as observers with the 20-man ambush team.

The evening of the ambush, Medford and I were shouldering our lightened rucks and guns, when Stotka walked up to us.

"I'm going to put the major beside you," he said. "I want you guys to take care of him. Make sure he doesn't do anything really strange."

The middle-aged major, whose slight paunch betrayed one too many desk assignments, was decked out in perfectly fitting, newly issued fatigues and gear. All shiny. He seemed excited, like an uncle who had received a rare invitation to a family camping trip.

The major walked between us as our party headed past the wire and down to the bamboo thicket. We were assigned positions in an L-shaped configuration along the trail. As quietly as possible, each man made a hide for himself under low brush or in the tall grass. The major was to the right of me and Medford.

As darkness settled in, we spread out our ponchos on the ground and reclined on them, belly down, guns pointed down the trail. We spoke in inaudible whispers. The ambush was serious business and surprise was critically important.

The silence was broken by a rhythmic, whooshy, wheezy farting sound. The fucking major was blowing up his fucking air mattress! In the dark! At an ambush! He was going to settle in and make a nice evening of the whole thing.

"Hey, don't do that, you goddamn stupid shit." I thought it. Medford thought it. But neither of us said it. The major happily kept blowing.

Soon we heard someone shuffle in beside us. It was the lieutenant.

"Who's making all the goddamn noise?"

"It's the major," I whispered.

"Huh. Oh, yeah," Stork replied. Then, a little louder, he added, "You people quiet down here" before taking off.

By then, the mattress was inflated. The major slept on it, soundly, while the rest of us kept our eyes peeled for the enemy. Whenever the major moved, Medford and I—and, presumably, everyone else within 40 feet—cringed to hear the squeaky rubber-and-air sound peculiar to air mattresses. And when the major wasn't stirring, he was snoring. In the middle of the night, he rolled over onto Medford.

Medford yelped.

The major groggedly cursed.

By the end of the noisy night, no one was taking the ambush seriously. We trudged back up the hill at first light. Our guests, disappointed at not seeing any action, piled into a helicopter and took off for some hot grub and showers at HQ. The ambush team slept most of the day away.

More spit than polish

The crisp fatigues of the visiting officers had accentuated our increasingly unregulated appearance. Since I'd left the spit-and-polish atmosphere of Fort Lewis, I'd been aware of a drop in the levels of concern over appearance at each stop along the way to the bush. On the firebase, there was decidedly more spit than polish. A quick dowsing in a jury-rigged shower was the most cleansing we could manage. Some men, including me, made do with the few streambed baths we enjoyed on our forays into the bush.

Laundry was done at the rear and returned in huge duffel bags. We gathered around the bags like women at a bargain basement table, grabbing for shirts and pants. We stripped, tossed our exceedingly grungy, sun-faded uniforms into a smelly mound and tried on clean fatigues that looked as if they might fit. This grab-bag approach was a losing proposition for big guys like me. Sleeves hit my wrists, pant legs reached my ankles.

Laundry was supposed to be choppered in weekly, but more pressing missions could keep the helicopters away from such housekeeping chores for two or three weeks. So the firebase was constantly littered with socks and shirts hung out to dry. Some guys fought a diligent but losing battle to remain hygienic in that dirt-lined broiling pan. Others made a joke of their uncouth state. They figured the predatory bugs that could stand the smell and get close enough to bite would never be able to chomp through the layer of dirt on their preys' bodies. That theory held true in the airless bunkers, at least, where the reek was usually so bad only the GIs would crawl in at night.

When I wrote to my mom that the men didn't wear anything under their pants in the interest of staying cool, she must have misinterpreted. She sent me two packages of underwear, lest I be indecent. I was delighted. The soft, clean cotton made excellent rags. While the other men spent their free afternoons sunbathing, I parked my fair-skinned carcass in the shade and cleaned weapons with J.C. Penney's finest jockey shorts.

My folks also sent me art materials to help fill my idle moments. I would sit with my back against a bunker, sketch pad resting on my knees, and capture the soft jungle landscape and harsh living conditions with colored pencil lines. Once, Stotka walked over and broke my concentration.

"So you can draw, huh? Well, I've got a project for you."

I spent the next two days designing a logo for the squad and penciling it onto most of their helmet covers.

The logo nurtured our (Stotka's) notion that we were "Killer, Warrior Grunts," something better than your run-of-the-mill grunts. It featured the words "The Ratpack"— Stotka's pet name for his unit—and the picture of a skull over two crossed, bloody bayonets.

The skull symbolized the squad mascot, Nguyen.

Nguyen had been an NVA soldier, identified by the name scratched on the flask-like canteen carried on what was left of his body. Stotka found him on the squad's most recent beyond-the-wire policing. Stotka was pleased to think that this particular soldier was one he might have killed in the running firefight as Charlie Company pulled of the firebase months earlier.

Stotka had cleaned the front half of the skull, which was intact, and carried it in his gas mask. He told the others in the squad that, according to local (his) custom, the skull was a good luck charm. Before leaving on a mission, he would pull the mask from its pouch, the skull's eye sockets staring vacantly from behind the goggles. Everyone was allowed to take a nibble out of Nguyen, chewing a bit of bone in hopes it would bring them invincibility and success in battle.

Not everyone wore the helmet logo. Such a display wasn't to the taste of Newton and Niederfringer, who wandered around the firebase with pants rolled up in the style of the Vietnamese peasants.

But the heart of the squad—the men whose exploits particularly pleased Stotka and whose appearance particularly embarrassed the battalion commander—wore the skull logo atop their increasingly diverse, non-regulation attire. There was an equally wide array of hair. Longest's Fu Manchu moustache and goatee grew luxurious. Laney's beard was sprouting like an organic Brillo pad. I sported a scrawny but determined red growth under my nose.

Everyone had a good luck charm. For Stotka, it was Nguyen; for Longest, love beads. For me, it was a thunderbird charm that Dave Mueller's dad had carried on campaigns in Italy and Japan during World War II. It hung next to my own dad's trusty P-38 can opener on a necklace I'd braided out of multicolored shoe laces.

Lynch's charms were two shotgun shells, one red and one green. They decorated his bush hat, where they remained even after that day when an officer flew to the firebase to inform the squad leaders that, due to a new policy of reasonably strict adherence to the Geneva Convention rules of warfare, shotguns were now outlawed in the bush.

Lynch took the news badly. A shotgun was like an extension of the hands for point men like Lynch. It allowed them to spray a lot of rounds in a general direction at short range and then get the hell out.

To these guys, the Geneva Convention sounded like a high-falutin' excuse to take away a comfortable, effective weapon. Besides, was the maiming done by this war's million land mines any less horrible than the wounds inflicted by double-ought buckshot? There was nothing Lynch could do, except do his best to use up every shotgun shell on the base before they came the next day to take away his Ithaca. I joined him and a small crowd, at the official garbage dump (not to be confused with the dump every squad created in front of its bunkers) and we pumped in the neighborhood of 400 rounds through Daisy, as Lynch affectionately called it. We shot at everything that moved and a lot of things that didn't. A monkey that had the poor timing to inhabit a tree in Lynch's line of fire got seriously blasted. It was the first creature that I saw killed in Vietnam.

A good puppy

The second killing I witnessed was of Stotka's black puppy, Bitch.

Bitch was one of millions of dogs that ran as wild as field mice all over Vietnam.

She was a good puppy, a generally pleasant nuisance. Stotka fawned and simpered over that pooch as a mother would her first-born. He cuddled her, played with her, and tolerated her puppy-ness.

It was breakfast time. The squad headed for the chow line, most of the men with M-16s slung over their shoulders. As usual, I wore my .45, pleased that I could carry the weight of the weapon on my hips, leaving hands and arms free.

Our dining hall was the ground around the flagpole, which stood in the middle of the firebase near the command hooch. We began to wolf down our ham and eggs.

Bitch sat at Stotka's feet, eyeing our food and hoping for her usual handout. I sat to Stotka's left, opening my carton of milk and talking with the man on the other side of me. I didn't notice Stotka slipping the rifle off his shoulder and casually aiming it at Bitch's head.

Stotka pulled the trigger. The dog's brains exploded in my direction.

We all looked at Stotka in open-mouthed disbelief. The sound of the point-blank shot brought people running out of the command hooch.

"What the hell is going on?" an officer demanded.

"The dog had rabies," Stotka replied as he picked up the plate he'd put down. "I saw her foaming at the mouth."

"I didn't see her foaming at the mouth!" I bellowed. "Look at my meal!"

I shoved the plate at Stotka. Globs of bloody gray tissue were splattered over the untouched eggs.

The officers walked away, shaking their heads. I lost my appetite. The whole squad was mortified by Stotka's act. We took it with the grizzled attitude of soldiers, but it still didn't make any sense.

The incident tarnished Stotka's golden boy image. Not long after the shooting, Stotka assigned Medford to another bunker and moved in with me. He evidently wanted me to be his understudy. Whatever the case, I was able to follow Stotka's orders and occasionally admire his bravado without making a religion out of either.

My fourth and final week on Firebase 30 was stagnant. The only excitement I felt was during a little firepower demonstration.

I and six other relative newcomers were in the trench that went through my bunker. We were wearing our flak vests and helmets. We took turns acting as forward observers, calling in fire support from the 81mm mortars and a 105mm howitzer. The mammoth 105s fired from a sister firebase two kilometers away.

The fire mission commands given over the radio were designed to help the infantry by targeting the guns on enemy positions. The commands were simple and effective, the artillery responded according to the basic training manuals.

"Blue dog 12, Blue dog 12," we radioed. "This is 32 Charlie."

"Fire mission," came the reply.

"Grid 763248, Direction, 130, distance 2100 drop 200."

"15-man patrol."

"Adjust fire."

"On the way."

Within seconds, a marker round would explode into smoke on the next hill.

Because the round wasn't likely to be on target—the gunners were like blind men playing darts, with only verbal clues to guide their aim—the commands would be adjusted.

"Raise five-zero, over."

"Roger, five-zero, on the way."

And the round would come in 50 meters further up the hill.

When the forward observer saw a marker round land where he wanted it, he said "Repeat, HE," and high explosives would fall. If he told the artillery to "fire for effect," the shells would rain down. The practice session stopped short of that. One false coordinate and we would have been blasted into Cambodia. As it was, the explosive rounds came too close for comfort. Shrapnel whizzed past our heads and the earth shook as the shells fell 100 yards or so down the hill.

By the time of the artillery session, some of the short-timers had already been shipped to the rear. Laney, for instance, was off to spend his last four months at a job he'd been trying to finagle for eight months: lifeguard on the Cam Ranh Bay beach.

About Jan. 18, 1969, the company got orders to move out. Because the last evacuation of the firebase had turned into a siege, we were apprehensive that it would mean four or five days of constant mortaring. More to the point, we hoped that whoever was responsible for dispensing the orders wasn't letting the North Vietnamese know about them.

For the most part, we were glad to be leaving the boredom.

Certainly, the apprehension we all felt wasn't enough to set off an emotional outburst in the usually mild-mannered Medford.

He and I were working side by side, destroying bunkers in preparation for the company's departure. We were using pickaxes and shovels to tear the planks and sandbags to pieces. When I gave 5-foot-4 Medford a needling for not being able to reach the highest sandbags in a pile, the young Southerner exploded. He started punching me on the chest, a reaction that was more than a little out of hand. It was hardly the first time he'd been called a short little shit.

I figured Medford, who was newly married and frustrated, must've gotten a letter from home that set his nerves on edge. So I didn't fight back. I just laughed as he pounded on me, which incensed him more. Finally, Stotka pulled Medford off and told him to go help the others carry supplies down to the LZ. Medford wandered off almost calmly, apparently having let off enough steam.

Hawk comes back

Jan. 20 was a day filled with the drone of helicopters. Choppers came in to carry out men and supplies. Gunships circled in case of trouble, but everything went smoothly.

I spent much of the morning sorting through the paraphernalia that had accumulated in my month there. Pencils and paper, clothes, candy bars, letters, flares, grenades, two cans of ammo, gun cleaning kit, extra M-60 barrel. What I couldn't throw out went into, or was tied to, my ruck. It ended up weighing a good 110 pounds. It was so heavy that, once it was on my back, I couldn't get up. So I held out my machine gun for Longest to grab and pull me to me feet.

I used the weapon as a crutch to balance the weight of the pack as I hiked down the trail. My platoon, the last to leave, was waiting at the helipad. I walked to the edge of the clearing, turned my back to the hillside and eased the pack onto the higher ground. I slipped off my flak vest, which was intertwined with the pack straps, and eased the weight off my back. I walked over to the other guys. They sat eating chocolate bars and wiping their faces to remove the dust kicked up by the incessantly whirring chopper blades.

There were only a handful of us left when Stotka looked up at the helicopter that was floating down to take us out.

"It's him, look! He's back from leave! It's our boy!"

Everyone's eyes followed Stotka's pointed finger. The veterans started yelling.

"It is him, out-fucking-standing, I knew he'd be back!"

The chopper dropped straight toward us, its skids coming within five feet of our heads. It banked to the left, soared, then nearly stalled. It dropped like a stone then, suddenly, turned into a feather. It made the smoothest, lightest landing I'd ever seen.

Through the plexiglass door window, I could see the pilot throw back his head and laugh hysterically, delighted with his own aerial acrobatics. Until he took his helmet off—revealing a bald head and his most distinctive features, a long, hawked nose and a white scarf, worn tied around his neck.

"Holy shit, man! Man, we knew you'd be back!" Guys were walking hunched over under the rotating blades to the pilot door, which Hawk had opened, and were giving him the soul fist and patting him on his head.

After a brief bit of banter, Hawk squawked, "C'mon, let's go!" and we started to pile our shit and us into the rocking Huey.

I was one of the last to get on. I backed up to the chopper and deposited the weight of my pack onto its floor. Medford helped pull me in.

Two gunners were behind M-60s in their own little seats at the back of the ship.

In the front, Hawk was laughing uproariously at someone's joke while his co-pilot sat calmly beside him, smoking his pipe and gazing out the window. Three of the eight passengers were in the center. The rest of us sat to the sides with our feet dangling out the open cargo doors.

"Hold on!" hollered Hawk.

Whopp, whopp, whopp, the chopper sprang off the ground, moving backward and to the side. I instinctively looked around for something to grab.

"Hey, don't worry," yelled someone behind me. "You don't have to hold onto anything. Centrifugal force will hold your ass in."

The former firebase shrank away from us. Before long we were cruising at 2,000 feet, the wind pushing my dangling feet and the chopper's rhythm vibrating me toward the door. As I involuntarily moved closer to the edge, several hands grabbed my flak vest and pulled me toward the center. The ride was more fun than frightening—until Hawk made a sharp turn.

I started sliding out, fast. I was about to grip a door handle when the door gunner turned around and pulled me in. Then the gunner slapped my wrist, pointed to the handle and gestured "NO." I shrugged, palms out, gesturing back "SORRY." Again, I scooted to the center of the chopper. Grabbing on to a pair of legs for security, I lay back and watched the undulating hilltops as Hawk took us to wherever the hell we were going.

Hawk

Chapter 12: Combustion Charlie

The month at Firebase 30 had turned me into a seasoned soldier, by virtue of boredom and dirt, if not by combat experience. I wasn't just another kid in uniform, a fresh fish. I was part of Charlie Company.

The choppers landed near another tired-looking firebase. From there, we were transported in a convoy that squeezed together and stretched out like an accordion as it moved toward a place called Blackhawk.

Like other machine gunners in the convoy, I was positioned at the front of the truck bed with my M-60 balanced on the cab. Like the guys sitting on sandbags behind me, I was in a buoyant mood, glad to be rid of the firebase and enjoying the sights and sounds of the increasingly busy road.

We turned onto a highway that buzzed with Army trucks, cars, carts and motorcycles. I was surprised that the route didn't seem to be guarded. It was a matter-of fact thoroughfare lined with huts and pedestrians whenever it wound through a town.

As the convoy reached the outskirts of Kontum, throngs of children rushed up to the trucks, hands extended for food or anything soldiers could spare. I thought of the war movies where smiling GIs would toss candy bars to European urchins. That wasn't going to happen here. If any of us had candy, we weren't about to throw away such coveted loot. Instead, we tossed out olive-green cans of ham and limas, eggs and sausage and John Wayne cookies (aka C-ration biscuits).

Once past the hassle and the honking of the cycle-filled market district, the convoy proceeded smoothly. It arrived at Blackhawk in late afternoon. Blackhawk was a tent-filled brigade or battalion center without such amenities as officers' clubs and billets. Like Dak To, it was flanked by mountains. The trucks drove to one side of the base, formed a circle like a wagon train and dropped us off. Charlie Company was to occupy a semi-circle of dry land at the side of the road.

Next to the road was the command post; behind that, and at the heart of the semi-circle, was an old French minefield surrounded by barbed wire. Next to the field were parts of a fort, including a tumbledown blockhouse surrounded by sandbags so old they turned to powder when touched.

Each platoon was assigned a wide wedge of land along the perimeter, so that the minefield was behind them and they faced out into a grassy field. I set up my M-60 above the defensive position that had already been dug next to the field, then joined Medford in putting up our shelter—Stotka was staying temporarily with our platoon folks—and we were pleased that we didn't have to dig foxholes. It was work enough pounding tent stakes into the sun-baked earth.

Guys were smoking and quietly talking as they set up camp. Suddenly, the calm was shattered by four explosions.

We all dived for our guns and began laying down a field of fire into growth at the perimeter edge.

"Cease fire! Cease fire!" someone yelled.

With my hands still on the M-60, I looked over my shoulder to see if someone had wandered into the minefield. Nothing of the kind.

Word spread quickly that Newton and Niederfringer had outsmarted themselves. Why drive in tent stakes, they figured, when they could use putty-like C-4 plastic explosives and blow little holes in the tough dirt and insert the stakes? The whole company was pissed. Infantrymen are trained to react to unusual fire as if it is from the enemy. With all the scrambling and shooting, someone could easily have been killed. Newton and Niederfringer had gone too far.

Seething, the platoon sergeant marched them around the minefield toward the command bunker. Behind the bunker was an old bomb crater. Capt. DeHart was summoned. A crowd began to form around the edge of the crater as the CO descended into it.

When I joined the audience, DeHart was berating Newton and Niederfringer with the vigor of a drill sergeant and the disdain of Gen. Patton. The duo were nervous and straight-backed—it was the first time I'd seen anyone stand at attention on a battlefield in a bomb crater. The transgressors were busted down to E-1 and told to get their goddamn butts back up to their squad and straighten up. [3]

Newton and Niederfringer shuffled in silence back to their area.

After Medford and I set up our tent, we helped clear a field of fire in front of our position. We waded into the tall grass and scrubby bushes and began hacking away with machetes. We worked side by side, trying to outrace the others who were also slashing away 35 or 40 feet of vegetation. We were almost finished when we smelled smoke. The field burst into a conflagration. Twenty-foot flames were sweeping toward us from the right. We scrambled back to our area and watched helplessly as the fire fanned toward the left and devastated the fourth platoon.

Tents caught on fire. Clothing caught on fire. Ammunition went off, wounding soldiers as they tried to escape. I began running alongside the orange wall of flame, yanking at people pawing through their stuff, yelling at them to get out, get out. Stotka joined me, dashing through the black, oily smoke and yelling. The fire outran us. Within minutes, it had reached the road where, out of fuel, it sputtered away to nothing. Stotka and I headed back through the destruction.

Men were sifting the ash, eyes straining through the smoke to find salvageable equipment. I grimaced as I saw what remained of fourth platoon's M-60, which was being cleaned when the fire hit. Its parts, neatly lain on the remains of a towel, were bent and scattered by booted feet. Then I saw a bandoleer of ammunition, strung with

---

[3] Don Newton recalls only that, on one occasion, he (and not Warren Niederfringer) was temporarily demoted. And that his offense was using dynamite to blast, rather than dig, a foxhole.

grenades and smoldering. Stotka saw it, too. He cursed and covered the hot grenades with a helmet that was lying nearby. Just as he stood up, the grenades blew. The force of the explosion picked him off his feet. A flying piece of helmet liner hit him on the head and knocked him unconscious.

I was knocked down, too. Flat on my back, I watched the helmet spiral upward until it was nothing but a dot in the gray sky. Then it dropped, a charred black mess with the top blown out of it, and crashed down beside my head.

I found my feet, stepped over the hole where the bandoleer had been and tried to rouse Stotka. I called for a medic, who arrived in short order and began slapping and washing the squad leader's face.

Stotka came around. His eyes were clear and he could talk, but he seemed confused. The medic led him away.

I returned to the second platoon's area and checked my equipment, which, along with Medford's, had been spared. Next door, fourth platoon members were fighting small fires with towels and pouring water from canteens on everything that was hot. Officers were ordering them to get out before more ammunition exploded. As I stood dabbing my bloody nose, a gray-haired master sergeant from the third platoon dashed past. The sergeant's wild-eyed face and uniform were soot black and he was screaming at the top of his lungs. He leapt over the barbed wire and began running through the mine field.

The sergeant was oblivious to the men who gathered near the wire, screaming "Get out of there, stop it, you're gonna get killed!" He ran in circles, blathering like an idiot. There was no telling what made him lose control.

At that point, a rocket launcher pack exploded from the heat. Hundreds of rockets, each containing riot gas, whooshed through the air.

"Hit the dirt! Fire in the hole! Run! Run!"

Everyone scattered. The berserk sergeant kept pounding around until one of the rockets hit him on the head. He collapsed in the center of the mine field.

Riot gas was mixing with the smoke from the fire. I ran to get my gas mask, as did most people who were still on their feet.

Into the chaos drove trucks, hauling in men to help clean up and hauling out the wounded. In the middle of it all, four soldiers clambered over the barbed wire and crawled toward the fallen sergeant, using their bayonets to prod the earth for mines. I stood watching their progress and washing the taste of gas from my mouth with a warm beer that someone in the squad handed to me. Within forty minutes, the mercy mission had succeeded and the breeze that had fanned the flames had also cleaned the air.

As the unconscious sergeant was rescued, everyone was speculating about what started the fire. We heard it was Newton and Niederfringer trying to clear away grass by burning it instead of cutting it. Whatever the cause, Combustion Charlie's reputation lived on.

I walked through the fourth platoon's area, surveying the damage. Five men had been hurt; almost all of the personal gear and equipment were gone. The machine gun that was destroyed was the one that was damaged at Christmas. It had been repaired for a week and a half. Once again, I had the only operational M-60.

I hadn't bathed in three weeks and, after the fire, was particularly pleased to learn that Blackhawk had a shower hall. With 20 or 30 shower heads, wooden benches and pegs for clothes, it was like the YMCA. Though I was disappointed to find that my first-ever suntan actually was a layer of red dirt that dribbled down the drain, I emerged refreshed. I put on my dirty fatigues and headed out the door.

As I left the shower hall, I recognized a private from advanced infantry training. We shook hands. He explained that he'd volunteered for long-range recon patrols and went into the bush for two or three weeks at a time.

After we chatted, he turned back to a conversation he had been having with some friends. They were discussing how they'd obtained the services of a young Vietnamese woman outside one of the tents at Blackhawk.

"Aw, she wasn't any goddamn good," one of them piped up. "I couldn't get her to do anything."

"Well, you should have done what l did," another said. "I moved her over in the rocks, made her uncomfortable, then she moved around a lot."

I listened with interest for a few minutes.

Then, tired by the frantic day and soothing shower, headed back to my tent for some sleep.

The burden of virginity

The next afternoon, Charlie Company moved to a rest area at another part of Blackhawk. The bunkers there were neat and clean, veritable Hilton rooms compared with the holes on the firebase. Because the area was secure, for the first time in recent memory, we didn't feel the need to wear helmets or carry weapons—except, of course, when an officer was looking.

A quarter-mile from the bunkers was a river where, I heard, I could wash my clothes. I sauntered down the road to its banks and found what was more social center than laundry. The vicinity was awash with humanity. Upstream, where 40-foot cliffs overlooked a deep pool, naked GIs took turns swinging Tarzan-style from a rope that was tied to a tree limb. They would let go of the rope, dive or jump as theatrically as possible, then climb back up the muddy bank for another swing. On the opposite bank, girls wearing yellow giggled at the soldierly antics as their mothers washed clothes and their fathers sold trinkets. The Americans who weren't splashing and hollering were drinking and catching some rays.

I turned downstream, where a series of shallow rapids preceded a small waterfall. I stripped, squatted on the rocks and began beating and wringing the dirt from my clothes. The sun and effort made me thirsty. When I finished, I bought two beers from a peddler. One can went into the pocket of my open shirt, the only clothes I was wearing. I downed the other as I waded around, wet pants flung over my shoulder, and drank in the carnival atmosphere and forest-framed scenery.

I'd just downed the second beer when a soldier on the shore signaled me.

"Hey! Hey, you, come here."

I walked over to him.

"Hey, there's a mamasan over there that's puttin' out real well," the guy said. He was zipping his trousers.

I was still a virgin, a fact that weighed on my mind a little. Yeah, I thought, maybe it's time.

"Where is this?"

"Over there," the GI answered, nodding toward a clump of trees that was downstream, just beyond the river fording site.

I thanked him and splashed along to where guys were waiting in line. I stepped onto the bank and joined them. The guy in front of me turned around, smiled and silently handed me a cigarette. I took a drag on the smoke and began counting the men from where I stood to where the front of the line disappeared into the bushes.

There were more than twenty awaiting the services of ... just one woman? "Uh, how many of them are there in there?" I asked the soldier who'd given me the cigarette.

"Oh, I don't know. I heard there's at least one."

The line moved slowly forward. In twenty minutes, I'd reached the bushes. I wasn't feeling particularly aroused and, when I saw and smelled human excrement on the ground, decided my introduction to sex would have to wait. I was about to gag.

"Excuse me, excuse me," I said as I wove my way through the guys behind me and returned to the river. I went back to where I'd left my boots. Sitting on a rock, I washed my feet, pulled on my pants and boots, and headed back to the bunker. I sat there for a long while, thinking about how I hated to be a pansy about something as commonplace as whoring, but good God! Stotka, who had quickly recovered from his altercation with the hot grenades, returned with my two other bunker mates of the moment. The four of us were lounging around, drinking beer and talking, when the company's new medic jumped through the doorway. He had sandy hair, glasses, pimples and what the troops viewed as an insulting preoccupation with their genital health.

"Have you been down to the river yet?" he demanded of no one in particular.

"No, not yet," someone mumbled.

"Well, when you go, don't forget to wash your foreskins."

He turned and leapt out of the bunker, kicking up dust as he went.

"You little sonofabitch," Stotka yelled.

"Yeah, you pervert!" added someone else, throwing comic books in the direction of the departed visitor, who was well on his way to being razzed out of the next bunker.

We stayed at the rest area for another day. On the second afternoon, I watched a demonstration of firepower from a nearby duster—a tank mounted with anti-aircraft guns. We didn't know what, if anything, the duster was firing at, but we found it to be an exciting display as the pom-pom guns dusted the surrounding bush with tremendous amounts of ammunition. With the ka-pom-pom-pom of the rounds, multicolored tracers arced through the air in graceful counterpoint to the destruction of the landscape.

The convoy

Word came down that we were going on a convoy in the morning, heading out for a major operation south of Blackhawk. The Army hoped to trap a North Vietnamese battalion in a hammer-and-anvil movement, and Charlie Company was to be the hammer. But first, we were to set up in an old French base camp in the boon toolies. The usual rumors abounded: By God, we told each other, we're finally going to see some action.

We were nervous—not about the possibility of battle, but about the convoy. This time, we would be on a dirt road, not a major highway. We would be vulnerable to an enemy who had perfected the business of attacking a convoy by boxing it in. The North Vietnamese would let the tank and armored personnel carrier at the front of the convoy pass by. The NVA then would detonate mines under the first and last trucks, forcing the convoy to stop, then open fire.

This tactic was such standard operating procedure that the GIs who were assigned to the first truck were the subjects of much pity. Or self-pity.

"Jeeeeeeeeesus H. Christ, we're doomed!" was the consensus in my squad when we heard that our truck was the first in line. We'd be easy pickings for the NVA. "What a chickenshit way to go!"

Our only hope was to get on the road early, before the enemy knew we were coming. But we didn't leave early, so we had plenty of time to contemplate that our number was up. We also had time and the means to get drunk, thanks to a grunt who bought whiskey down by the river.

About noon, after we piled some of the company supplies and ammunition into a trailer that our truck was pulling, we started drinking. Then we loaded ourselves into the truck. As the waiting and drinking went on, one of the men began using a radio in the truck to call other, equally bored GIs. Someone else produced a spotted camo parachute, ripped it into strips and made gaudy headbands for everybody. The whole squad looked like a den of Cub Scouts dressed like Indian braves.

The only sober person in the vicinity was a girl hawking sunglasses. She was about 11, not young enough to be cuddly-cute and not old enough to be feminine. She was all business, demanding five piasters for wraparound plastic sunglasses with paper-thin lenses. She aimed her sales pitch at Longest.

"You buy these. GI! You buy before you die, GI! You in first truck!"

"Kid, you get the hell out of here," Longest answered. "Little jerk!"

"No, GI, me just make fun. Me want sell sunglasses," the girl fired back. She never softened as she launched into a voracious argument. Or maybe I should say tenacious. Longest was no match for her. The other guys were growing fond of the kid. Somebody said, "Hey, man, she can flip shit back as fast as you can dish it out."

Longest snorted. He asked the girl: "Hey, kid, you boom-boom?"

"No, me no boom-boom."

"Well, you got a big sister?"

"No, no. No big sister."

"How about a little brother?"

"You no boom-boom my little brother, you dinky dow GI!"

That line got everybody clapping, and somebody said, "What the hell, let's buy some of the kid's sunglasses." And they all did, except for me. I couldn't, because I wore those thick prescription shades.

It was about 1530 hours when she made her last sale, and we finally started to roll. Our truck fell in behind the rattling tank and personnel carrier. As usual, I was on top behind the cab with the M-60. The edge of the forest came right down to the road. There was plenty of cover out there. Way too much cover.

We'd bounced along for 15 minutes, and the truck went around a bend. Just as it turned, I could see a tree that overhung the road. Men on top of the personnel carrier were ducking so they wouldn't get whacked. I reached for the machine gun to get it out of the way of the branches. I'd barely lifted it when the explosion hit. The concussion threw me against the cab, shoulder first. The other men—who'd been dangling their feet over the back of the truck, hiding behind the trailer as they passed around a bottle—were thrown on top of me. I couldn't catch my breath, couldn't see anything, could only hear groans.

Stotka yelled. "Get outta the truck, get outta the fucking truck!"

Men started falling over the sides. With their weight off me, I could get some air and get my bearings. I climbed over the cab to retrieve the M-60, which had fallen on the hood. Then I hopped off and joined everyone at the side of the road.

The mine had hit the trailer instead of the truck, nearly demolishing it. Amazingly, the explosion didn't set off any of the C-4, the dynamite, the TNT or the riot gas that was inside. No one was badly hurt, either, though the men who'd been in the back were complaining about splitting headaches. The driver, a big guy like me, was on the verge of a breakdown, shaking and crying. "I don't want to do this shit anymore, I can't handle it anymore."

I watched everybody running about, taking orders, and it struck me. Every polka-dot-bandannaed face I saw was covered with soot and wearing a pair of James Bond wraparound sunglasses—with no lenses. The explosion had popped the lenses right out of the chintzy frames. I was watching a bunch of pickaninnies in a bizarre comedy, and I laughed hard. I roared.

When I wiped the tears that were streaming down my face, the back of my hand got smeared with black. The rest of the squad just looked at me like I was the strange one.

Not one of them grinned back.

Quick service

A jeep full of officers took charge. Men in the next truck cordoned the area and searched unsuccessfully for the trip wire and the enemy who had detonated the mine.

Meanwhile, a medivac chopper appeared overhead and someone went into a nearby field and popped smoke to bring it in.

"My God, that's quick service," I said to no one in particular.

We were all pleased to think that help had arrived so soon, even though we didn't need it. But the chopper hadn't come for us. It had been summoned by the personnel carrier. One of the carrier's passengers who had ducked to avoid the overhanging limb had unthinkingly left his hands outside the hatch and had lost some fingers. He was being airlifted to a hospital.

My squad salvaged what it could from the trailer, then kicked and shoved its remains off the road. Before we could climb into the scorched truck and ride on, a scorched rocket launcher still hiding in the trailer exploded. The rockets landed harmlessly in the field.

Somewhat sobered, we reached our destination less than an hour after leaving Blackhawk.

We piled out and found ourselves at another remnant of the French occupation. But there was nothing white-pillared or grand about this dusty red death hole. A watchtower that looked like a huge anthill with its top chewed off looked down on the compound, which was surrounded by a mud wall.

We were told to form a perimeter outside the wall, with the expectation of moving out in a couple of days.

Stotka decided that the M-60 should be set up near an arched entrance in the wall, so he and I began to dig our foxhole there. While everyone else found it easy to dig foxholes and post holes for barbed wire, we hit nothing but rocks. I could almost hear the long-gone Gallic commander saying, "Mon Dieu, we're going to have a lot of trucks coming through this archway! Let's fill this path full of rocks for them."

Goddamn French.

Soon after we'd begun digging, Stotka ran off to a meeting to be briefed on the next day's activities. I kept shoveling. The late afternoon sun behind me was hot, so I took off my shirt and dug for an hour. The other guys gave me a lot of sympathy, but no help.

After I'd moved about a ton of rocks, I had a decent-sized foxhole. And a badly sunburned back, which worried me. In the Army, sunburn is considered destruction of government property. If I couldn't carry a pack and take part in the upcoming maneuver, I could be written up for property destruction or given an Article 15, which might mean a reprimand, extra duty, loss of pay. I could even be court martialed.

When Stotka saw my lobster back, he asked DeHart to take a look at it. The CO decided I should be sent to the rear—in this case, the camp at Landing Zone Blackhawk—to recuperate. Asking to stay, I picked up a loaded pack and put it on.

"See, I can carry it. It doesn't hurt."

It hurt like hell. But I didn't want to be sent to the rear. I wasn't the world's best soldier, but I wasn't the world's worst. I didn't want any disciplinary measures on my record.

DeHart didn't seem angry, but he held firm that I should fly out in the morning. So I went into the compound and pleaded my case with the chaplain. Who would hear none of it. I wouldn't be punished, they said, and I would be useful because I could carry some correspondence back to Blackhawk.

Still, I couldn't get rid of the nagging doubt that I was going to get an Article 15. I was standing around, probably looking forlorn, when a convoy was getting ready to move out with some support troops. The battalion doctor was in one of the trucks and the chaplain called him out to examine me. DeHart joined them.

"Take off your shirt, soldier," the chaplain said, turning from me to the doctor. "See, look at his back. And he wants to go out on a combat patrol."

I stood there surrounded by a major and two captains. They poked and prodded until I felt like a ham being inspected and found unfit for consumption.

"No, I don't think he should go," the chaplain said. When the doctor agreed, I started to speak.

"But chaplain, I..."

"Never mind, you just do as you're ordered. You won't be getting in any trouble. Just do your duty."

The discussion was over. I headed back toward my tent behind the foxhole, where I was approached by Calvin, a husky newcomer to the squad.

"Stotka came and talked with me and I'm supposed to take the machine gun," he said in a Southern drawl that was becoming very familiar. "Goddamn thing, I don't want to take that goddamn thing out there. It weighs too goddamn much."

"Well, I guess you don't have too goddamn much choice," I grumped back at him.

It was another replacement, known as the Undertaker, who made the evening memorable for me. He was my tent mate for the night and cheered everyone by sharing a care package he'd received from his dad, an airline pilot. The box included goodies from first class and single-serving bottles of liquor, all of which had to be consumed because they would be extra baggage to carry on the upcoming boonie-hump.

The Undertaker was about 20. He had a prominent nose, a heavy beard and a disarming fascination with death. Although he spoke with a New Jersey accent, he hailed most recently from Florida, where his stepfather ran a funeral parlor. He was called the Undertaker because that's what he was studying to become. He talked about bodies, about embalming, about the famous people he'd helped bury, about how he wanted to be pickled when his time came. He talked about death, death, and death. It was the last topic infantrymen want to dwell upon and, as a result, the Undertaker wasn't making many lasting friends.

Despite the constant deadly drivel, I could hardly pitch the guy out. Like all of the other sometimes-unsavory characters in the squad, he had become a buddy.

Morning came and I went. As I was crossing the LZ to the chopper, Stotka came running up to me with a puppy in his arms.

"Here, take care of Sparky and don't lose him, whatever you do," he said, thrusting the squirming animal at me. "He's my favorite dog."

"What are you talking about?"

"He might get killed out here. You take him and take real good care of him. Don't lose him! Don't let anything happen to him!"

Now I knew why Stotka had wanted me to go to the rear. My God. Another piddly-ass, urinating, defecating dog. I took it, turned, strode toward the waiting helicopter and shoved the dog inside the mailbags that filled the cargo area.

The pilot and co-pilot laughed and pointed at the slobbering puppy as the chopper lifted off. "He sure is a cute fucker, ain't he?" the pilot said over the roar of the blades.

When we landed at Blackhawk, I jumped out and shouldered the M-16 that I'd been traded. I put the dog under my left arm and picked up my pack with my free hand.

The chopper took off. Along with the usual storm of dust, it blew the struggling puppy out from under my arm.

"Come back, you stupid dog!"

The puppy, frightened by the helicopter, ran like mad into a bunch of tents. I rejoiced. He was gone. Then I remembered Stotka's orders. So I made a cursory search, wandering about in full combat gear, calling for "Sparky!" I gave up when I realized I was being stared at.

Mascot

Chapter 13: Rosemary's Baby and the traffic Gestapo

"Where's Charlie Company First of the Eighth's command hooch?" I asked one of the engineers who'd been staring at me. He directed me toward a tent with a California State flag flying above it.

It was the same tent that had been at Dak To when headquarters had been there, run by the same two young sergeants who had processed me into the company. The sergeants—a tall one with hair bleached surfer-white and a short one with dark hair—were Californians, which explained the flag. They welcomed me, pointed toward a cot and told me to put my gear there. Then they explained my duties. They talked as if I'd be there forever.

The first thing I did was wander down to the chow hall for a decent hot meal. When I got back, there was no one in the tent. I found some comic books and grabbed a beer from the refrigerator. I was thinking that the place might not be too bad when a young lieutenant stormed in.

"Who the hell are you?"

"Pvt. Myers, sir."

Then the lieutenant demanded to know where the white-haired sergeant was.

"I don't know, sir, I'm just here ... He told me to stay and answer the phone."

"Shut up, goddamnit, I don't want to hear anything from you. Tell that sonofabitch when he calls that I want to see him. I'm gonna have his ass."

The lieutenant ran out. I knew I'd just met the company martinet, although I had no idea why the guy was so hot under the collar.

The sergeant in question returned. I told him what had happened.

"Jesus Christ, you didn't tell him I was here, did you?"

"No, just that you were gone."

"Good God, he's after me now," he grumbled.

At that moment, the lieutenant came back.

"There you are! You sonofabitch, I'm gonna have you lined up..." and the two of them began a 10-minute shouting match. From what I could make of it, the sergeant was in trouble for failing to turn in a laundry slip.

The lieutenant, having vented his wrath at the sergeant, looked over at me.

"Get a shave and get your ass cleaned up. If you're going to be back here, you might as well look like a civilized human being."

Then he left.

I spent the rest of the afternoon getting clean, answering the phone and carrying supplies from one tent to another. After dinner, a helicopter flew in with eight men from the third and fourth platoons. There was no room for them in the company tent, or in any nearby. Finally, the white-haired sergeant escorted the exhausted soldiers to the chapel. Grateful for any place to crash, the GIs filed into the large tent with pews made of rough-hewn planks.

They were dozing off when the chaplain came by. Upset at the sight of them, he ran off and returned with the martinet.

"Who let these people sleep in here?" the lieutenant raged. "This is a house of the Lord!"

"These guys need a place to sleep. Can't you have the common decency to let them sleep?" the sergeant replied. "There's no place else for them."

"Let them sleep in the goddamn dirt. They're not sleeping in my chapel," said the lieutenant. The chaplain stood beside him, eyes averted from the argument.

The soldiers were too tired to complain. The sergeant took them to a tilted trailer that was behind the company tent. Three of them slept inside the trailer, the others clustered around it on the ground. They stayed there for a few days before moving on. At night, I would walk out with a flashlight to check on them, see if they needed anything.

Later that first night, someone in the battalion arranged to bring in a movie. It was going to be *Rosemary's Baby*, which they'd heard was big in the States. They set up a portable screen outdoors and put the projector on the hood of a jeep. A big, cigar-smoking sergeant major served as projectionist. Guys sat on folding chairs and oil drums, drank beer and enjoyed themselves until halfway through the first reel, when four or five riot gas canisters came whooshing into the screening area.

The canisters banged onto the jeep, knocking over the projector. The film reel rolled into the dirt. As gas seeped into the air, men scrambled for safety, toppling chairs and oil drums. I headed for the company tent but, by the time I got there, the two sergeants had already gone inside and zipped up the entrance. They didn't want to open it to let me in, so I crawled under the side, found my gas mask and crawled back out.

I looked back toward the jeep and saw nothing but overturned chairs and the whirring projector, which was throwing a beam of light through the riot gas.

The movie was canceled for the night. We couldn't get everyone back together, because a group of the incensed audience members were off retaliating against the engineers who had tossed the canisters.

The following evening, three of us joined a friendly motor pool sergeant in his tent. Using a white towel as a screen, we fed *Rosemary's Baby* back into the projector. We drank beer, smoked dope and watched the rest of the movie.

On my third day at Blackhawk, I was assigned to accompany a battalion buck sergeant on a laundry run into Pleiku. We took the battalion jeep, which the sergeant took care of very conscientiously—waxing and buffing it, even polishing the copper gasoline lines that led in and out of the carburetor.

Besides shining the jeep, the sergeant had polished the badge on his bush hat, removing the non-reflective black paint that was required at the front but was unnecessary here.

As I loaded the laundry into the back of the jeep, the shiny badge caught the eye of the lieutenant, who was walking past. He tore the hat off the sergeant's head and insisted that he go inside and put black paint back on the badge. The sergeant followed the order, but grumbled about it as we drove down the busy highway to Pleiku and Camp Enari, home of the 4th Infantry Division. When we got there, I carried the sacks into a laundry building that was as big as an aircraft hangar and packed with 40-foot mounds of clothes. Most of the Vietnamese workers there were kids. Dozens of them swarmed around me as I turned to head for the door. Their eyes got big. They ran to me, pointed and called their friends. I didn't know what the excitement was about until I heard some of them shout "Beaucoup! Beaucoup!" I must have been the largest human they'd ever seen.

I broke away from the crowd—the kids seemed disappointed that I didn't have goodies for them—and returned to the jeep.

We had five hours to kill before we were to pick up a consignment of clean clothes. We drove through Pleiku— a collage of outrageous signs in pigeon English, graceful women and men wearing white shirts and sunglasses—and went to the Air Force base for lunch. We checked in our weapons, which were tagged and put into a vault, like hats at a nightclub.

The base was full of sweet-looking American gals walking around in shorts, men in civilian clothes mowing lawns ... it looked like good old Mountain Home AFB, Idaho. But this place had something a military installation in the U.S. wouldn't have: soldiers of every flamboyant description. In addition to green berets, there were maroon, red and black berets. There were men in tiger-striped and camo-spotted fatigues; officers of every kind; even Australian troops whose bush hats tilted cockily to the side.

I felt a little out of place among the dashing dudes and mucky-mucks. But I noticed that, at the drive-in restaurant where we lined up to eat, everyone was eating off the same menu of milkshakes, steaks and beans. We grubbed down sitting at a picnic table and after getting a couple more shakes we headed off to see what there was to see in Camp Enari.

We drove past a theater building bearing the sign 4th Infantry Museum. It was open. We figured, "Why not?" and pulled in. There were testimonials and stuff from every battle in division history. I wandered about, thoroughly entertained by the chromed entrenching tool that dispatched 10 attackers; the chrome helmets with remarkable bullet holes in them; the weird weapons and foreign warrior garb and various things relating to tigers and jungle tiger attacks.

Posted on the wall just outside the restroom doors were giant cards handmade for our troops by grateful American students. They included one I had made for our boys in the 4th Infantry for Christmas of 1967, my brush strokes expressing the wonder of the season, or some such. Neat! I wanted to show my driver buddy, but he was out in the jeep raring to go.

It was late afternoon when we retrieved the laundry and headed back to Blackhawk. I was having fun. As we rolled through town, I sat in the passenger's seat, watching children beg food from truckloads of soldiers. I gave a smart salute to anyone who might be an officer. Before long, we were on the highway, humming along at 60 miles an hour. The speed limit was fifty and, before long, the sergeant cursed.

"Oh, shit," he said, glancing in the rear view mirror. "They're after me."

I looked over my shoulder. Sure enough, a truck was barreling down at us. Then it was beside us. The driver waved a weapon and signaled us to pull over.

The truck pulled in front. Six MPs jumped out and surrounded the jeep, their weapons pointed in the air. Another policeman, still in the truck, trained his M-60 on me and the sergeant. "Do you know how fast you were going?" demanded the traffic team's apparent leader. "Show me your IDs."

As the MPs inspected our cards, rubbing them to make sure they weren't counterfeit, I murmured to the sergeant, "What the hell is this?"

"Oh, I gotta put up with this every time."

The ringleader delivered a ticket and a stern lecture on the evils of speeding before he and his Gestapo jumped in their truck and sped off. "That's unbelievable," I croaked, "They treated us like deserters or gooks."

"Yeah, they're like headhunters. They pounce on you for the least possible reason. I was going fifty-seven or fifty-nine. Now I have to pay a $20 fine or get an Article 15 or a court martial or something."

The sergeant started the engine and drove back to Blackhawk at a compromise speed of 55.

I spent the night on bunker guard with a bunch of nervous soldiers who sent a flare or grenade into the pitch darkness every time they heard a bush crackle or a tin can rattle. I got no sleep.

My jobs the following day included rebuilding the fourth platoon's M-60. With a few new parts and a few salvaged from the fire, it went together fairly smoothly and functioned well on the firing range.

I was never ordered to see a doctor about the state of my back, which was peeling and tender but healing. On my fifth day at Blackhawk, I was told to hang around the LZ, where I could load cargo and wait for a ride out.

For the next three days, I loaded and unloaded food, mail, medicine and water.

Three of us awaiting rides worked under a most obnoxious sergeant. One morning, he gave one of his regular helpers a particularly nasty chewing out, then ordered him to the base to get some beer. Then the sergeant walked out to the middle of the LZ to ready a water tank trailer for airlifting. It was a job he insisted upon doing himself "so it will damn well get done right."

He checked the huge filler cap on the tank, banging on the lid and fastening it down. He stood on the tank and attached the cables that were wrapped around it to a hook under the chopper that was hovering overhead. Then he jumped down and signaled the pilot that the tank was secure.

The helicopter lifted off. It was 15 feet above the sergeant's head when the trailer flipped upside down. The tank lid popped open and a ton of water cascaded down, washing the sergeant off the helipad into bushes and a tangle of barbed wire.

Those of us looking on broke out laughing. The chopper, its pilot unaware of what had happened, kept ascending. It was 50 feet in the air when the cables broke and the trailer smashed into the red dirt where the sergeant had been standing.

With the chopper circling overhead, we helped our lacerated and subdued supervisor out of the barbed wire. As he wandered off toward the dispensary tent, his assistant ambled in, heard the story, laughed hysterically and passed around the sergeant's beer.

Chapter 14: Stiletto

When I finally got a ride out of Blackhawk, I was the only passenger. As I settled in among the cargo, the pilot turned and wordlessly offered me a cigarette. For the first time in Vietnam, I felt like a member of a club or, maybe, of a conspiracy.

Still, when I got back to my squad, it took a few days for me to recapture the camaraderie I'd felt with them. The operation they'd been on for the past week had been rather unsuccessful—only a handful of enemy known killed—but it was an adventure I hadn't shared. Still, they seemed glad enough to see me. Calvin, the replacement machine gunner, was especially pleased.

The company was at a new firebase that made Firebase 30 look like a city park. It was on a cone hill much closer to the Cambodian border and had been used by the South Vietnamese and French armies for years. The sandbags were made of chalky white canvas. Blown-up cannons and bullet-ridden helicopters were part of the scenery.

Worst of all, the place was hot. The top of the hill was actually a mound of trash that had been covered with dirt, like a compost heap. The refuse of countless soldiers had been burnt for years and now it smoldered beneath the troops. It was truly a firebase, a fitting home for Combustion Charlie Company, with smoke constantly seeping from underground.

The heat intensified the need for water, which was in short supply.

Until I arrived, the company had sent patrols to the river below to get water. But enemy activity was picking up in that vicinity—the GIs could even hear the roar of the elephants the NVA used to move equipment—and the patrols stopped going out. No one wanted to get shot for the sake of a full canteen.

The troops pinned their hopes on the helicopters, which they had asked to bring in a blivet, which was a large rubber bladder with a self-sealing hole that could be opened with a stick. It had a major drawback. If left in the sun for long, the rubber befouled the water. I told the guys not to expect any great relief, because the blivets I'd seen at Blackhawk sat around the entire time I was there.

I was pulling guard near the LZ when a blivet-carrying chopper arrived. It was just about to land when the blivet broke loose. I watched it smack into the ground and roll and bounce, gathering momentum, down the hill. Smash, roll; tear, crash, roll; smash ... It crashed along for five minutes, sending birds flying and monkeys chattering until it came to rest on the jungle floor.

The officers had to send out two patrols—one for water, one to destroy the blivet to keep the enemy from using it.

Headquarters promised to send in another blivet adding, with grand understatement, that this one wouldn't be as fresh as the first. The first soldiers to gather around it, eager to fill their canteens, nearly gagged as they drank what tasted like liquid rubber. Even mixing a cup of it with two packs of chocolate drink powder barely masked the nauseous smell and flavor.

The craving for fresh water was so intense that no one in my platoon was upset at being volunteered for a patrol down to the river. It was going to be the first patrol led by George, our new lieutenant. George—Stork's popular replacement—was a stocky Californian with a thick moustache that curled up on the ends.

He told us how he used to live on the third floor of a warehouse in L.A., how he was into the drug scene before he joined the Army. We were surprised to hear that. He seemed so mature, a natural officer.

That patrol, and the others that I went on during my three weeks on the firebase, took us through an eerie countryside. The land between the top of the hill and the jungle near the river was full of stunted, twisted trees and huge red mounds that were home to a strange variety of insects. We waded through multicolored grasses in territory that I could easily picture on the pages of *National Geographic*.

The only action we saw was through binoculars. We could spot airplanes strafing and firing rockets in the distant hills. At night, the planes appeared as silver flashes, like glimmers of light on a car windshield. During the day, brown puffs of dust would erupt from the bombs and we would wait a few seconds for the inevitable boom that followed.

One night, we sat on our bunkers and watched a B-52 strike mission in support of infantry operations. The tons of high explosives being dropped caused a blue and yellow arc of light across the horizon. The strike was maybe 20 miles away, but the air on the firebase seemed to vibrate from the deep rumbling sound.

I had yet to face the enemy, but dogs continued to give me grief.

To my relief, Stotka had not mentioned Sparky's failure to return from Blackhawk. For the moment, he was getting along without a dog. But Stiletto had adopted a puppy. Alas, the puppy had contracted what Stiletto thought was rabies. He wanted to put the puppy out of its misery.

Stiletto showed up at my bunker one evening.

"Can I borrow your .45? I want to kill my dog."

"You want to kill your dog?"

"Yeah. I want to kill my dog but I don't want to use my M-79."

"I can understand that," I said, imagining a grenade launcher aimed at that scrap of pooch. "Where are you going to do it?"

"Over there by the LZ on the temporary firing range."

"That's fine with me. We'd better call in and tell higher-ups what you're going to do so they don't get all excited when the rounds go off."

After he had radioed the command hooch, I handed my .45 to Stiletto.

"It's got eight rounds in it. Don't waste 'em. I've only got two clips. And don't blow your goddamned foot off."

"I won't."

Stiletto walked off, gun in one hand and a boxful of sick puppy in the other.

I returned to the letter I'd been reading.

Bam! I heard the .45 go off. Bam! Bam! Boom! Bam! Boom! Bam! Bam! I jumped to my feet. What was that crazy shit-fr'-brains doing? Stiletto wandered back in. He was shaking and could barely talk. He handed me the pistol.

"What the hell's wrong with you?"

Stiletto started blubbering.

"I ... I tried to kill him. I couldn't hit him, then I just wounded him."

"It took eight rounds?"

"Well, I closed my eyes. I couldn't..."

He couldn't go on.

Stiletto never quit quivering. The next day, he was violently sick. Everyone was worried that he was going over the edge. As the medics called in a helicopter for him, the rest of us packed his gear. We helped him into the chopper, which was filled with soldiers headed out, and handed him his helmet and a rifle. The last thing Stiletto did was reach into his pocket for the little silver camera he always carried. With shaking hands, he took a picture of his buddies.

The chopper took off and headed down the valley, but never reached its destination. We heard later that it simply disappeared.

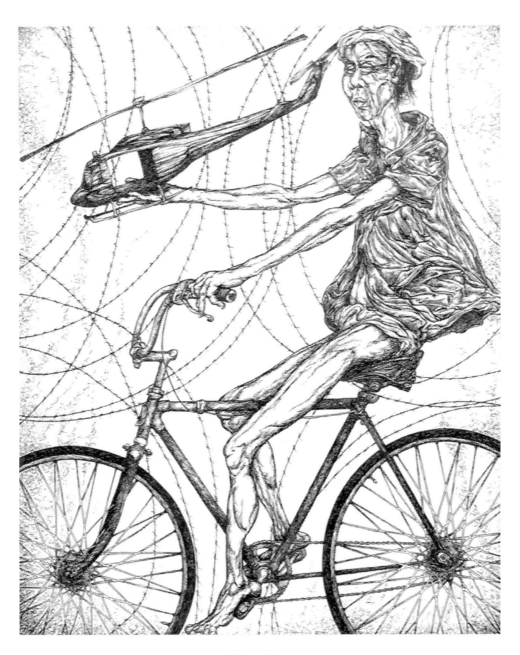

Toymaker

Chapter 15: The bowels of hell

An infantryman is rarely told more than he needs to know to do his job, and sometimes not even that.

When Charlie Company was lifted off its fuming firebase to the sound of enemy tanks in the valley below, rumor had it we would be perimeter guards at a new battalion firebase. We had also heard we would be part of a sweeping mission of some sort. As the choppers wafted us to brigade headquarters and a convoy waiting at a large LZ to transport us from there, we could only sit back and wait, stomachs churning with the anticipation of something we didn't know enough about to fear.

As the convoy moved out, I was back in my position, machine gun balanced on yet another truck cab. This time, it wasn't the lead truck. The convoy lurched and stopped all day. At one stop, at dusk, our truck was parked beside a small Vietnamese house that served as a kind of way station. Guys jumped down and asked the residents if they had any beer or soda, which they did. In fact, they had a refrigerator full of beverages for sale, as if they expected boocoo thirsty travelers. It was entirely possible that they knew more about the movement of American troops than the troops did.

Along with our beer, we ate coconuts that a boy tossed from a tree above the truck.

There were no kids in one village we passed. At least, none who were alive.

The place had been ransacked by the enemy. Although we drove by it quickly, we could see the grotesque outline of bodies hanging from a spiked fence that surrounded a central village compound.

The story came down that the bodies were those of children who had lived in the village orphanage. The French priest who was in charge had been killed before the children were murdered, dismembered and strung from the fence.

The convoy lurched on in the dark. It was a dangerous time to be on the road. The vegetation brushed my face as I looked ahead and saw foam hitting rocks as a river flowed across the road. I was nervous as the trucks lumbered across it, but the water was shallow and posed no problem.

It was the road that gave us trouble. Our driver misjudged its width in the dark as he rounded a curve and the right-side wheels ended up on a steep bank. A quick snap to the left and the truck tilted nearly onto its side. I managed to hold onto the M-60, but my helmet tumbled off my head and down a hill toward the river. It was followed by nearly half the squad's equipment and one soldier. The driver, who had climbed out onto the road, was shaking. Convoy truck drivers shook a lot.

Three guys retrieved their fallen comrade, their equipment and, to my disgruntlement, my helmet. I was hoping to be rid of the hot, heavy thing.

We righted the truck and headed into what looked more like an American deciduous forest than an Asian jungle. In the middle of the road, in the middle of the night, the trucks stopped. Someone walked by, banging on them.

"Get out, get out. Movin' out, saddle up."

We fell in line and started marching. There began a steady murmur.

"Where the fuck are we going?"

"I don't know."

"Hey, did you hear 'em say where we're headed?"

"Shut up and move out."

We walked single file along the road for a half hour, then turned into the forest.

We marched through the night up and down hills, sliding down river banks, wading through currents with weapons held overhead. At one point, we got lost and found ourselves walking in a circle. At another, we heard what we thought was the enemy. It was only by maintaining silence that we recognized rhythmic American bitching and cussing, and determined that the "enemy" was our own fourth platoon.

Just after dawn, we crossed a paddy and climbed to the top of a hill. It was a beautiful place with leaves covering the ground—more autumn-in-Vermont than winter-in-Vietnam. We were told to set up a defensive position.

"Dig in," Stotka said. "We're going to be here for awhile."

"Hell," I said, kicking up leaves. "I'd like to live in this place."

I found a rock formation that would provide a secure position for the M-60.

I'd barely begun to dig in behind it when Stotka came by.

"Let's saddle up, we're getting ready to move out. Choppers will be coming in to get us."

There were no choppers. So all of us—tired, disgruntled—headed out on the long trek back down through the forest and out to the road. Trucks arrived to take us a short distance to the new battalion area we'd heard about.

I didn't understand it. We'd slogged through a whole night's activity, apparently for nothing.

It was late afternoon before we reached the firebase, where we were shown to bunkers on the perimeter. I was among those who didn't have to pull the first shift of guard duty, so I lay down for the first sleep I'd had in a day and a half. My bunker was directly below a self-propelled howitzer, which was firing as I fell into my bunk. For all I know, it fired the rest of the day. When I woke up, I was covered with a pall of dust from the gun's constant recoil and movement on its tracks.

After the decrepit camps I'd seen, I found it interesting to watch the new base being built. On the second day, I was part of a patrol that guarded a group of chainsaw-wielding engineers who were cutting down trees for the construction. Every once in a while, one of the engineers sauntered over to us, shook his head and said, "Boy howdy, I'd sure hate to be in your shoes."

"Who the hell wants to hump around one of those goddamn saws and cut down trees all day?" was the usual reply.

I couldn't entirely understand the universal pity felt for the infantrymen. I gladly accepted the concern and the lunches that the engineers shared with their guards—even if I couldn't share with them the adventure I found in the infantry.

The company received some replacements while it was at the battalion camp.

My squad got two new soldiers. One was a nice kid from a Philadelphia ghetto, our first black since Laney left. The other was a dud.

The slow-looking fellow had already plagued the Army, which had shouted at, reprimanded and busted him as often as it could. Or so the story went. Now he plagued his fellow infantrymen, who knew what it meant when one of their ranks didn't shoulder his own load. If he was slow to react, as this guy was, or fell asleep on guard, as this guy did, it was more than a matter of "you're causing a lot of problems" or "you're going to get fired." The consequence of not doing the job could be someone's death. So my buddies and I began taking on the dud's responsibilities. Short of taking him out and shooting him, we didn't know what else we could do.

Next, the squad fell victim to a company-wide scourge of diarrhea. It left no one untouched. For two days, a circle of pale-looking men took turns at the open-air toilet.

We were regaining our strength by the fourth or fifth day, when we moved out again.

This convoy, which took us past Blackhawk, deposited us at dusk in a beautiful little valley. The lush grass was knee high, the flowers were bright and the stream was clear in the meadow where we camped.

The company established a perimeter on the base of the encircling hills. For the next two hours, the guards watched the lovely meadow turn into a parking lot filled with armored personnel carriers, cannons and trucks loaded with troops and equipment.

We loaded into the trucks the next morning. This was only a short hop. We arrived at an airfield, driving onto its long tarmac strip through a gate flanked by mines and barbed wire. The huge black field—surrounded by wire-topped chain link fence but no gun posts—was crowded with thousands of men. There were few tents. Guys were sleeping on the ground or huddled around cook stoves.

As soldiers milled around one end of the field, a C-123 landed at the other end, loading and unloading Vietnamese civilians. The hundreds of passengers who deplaned melted into the crowd that had gathered outside the fence. The Vietnamese had their usual plethora of items for sale. Some of them even reached through the chain link, offering their wares to the soldiers who were squatting to defecate in the relative seclusion at the edge of the field.

The most unusual peddler was also a pedaler, a loin-clothed Montagnard who somehow made his way through the gate the next morning on a Japanese bicycle. In one hand, he held aloft a helicopter model that he had carved out of balsa wood. We were mesmerized by the toy chopper, which was perfectly scaled from its skids to its three-foot blades. When the bicycle stopped, soldiers gathered around it. They pulled out rolls of money and began to bid on the model. What a great souvenir.

I reached for my money, too, then instantly thought better of it. What would I do with the goddamn thing? I could hardly carry it in my pack, and we were due to move out on an operation. The peddler looked around with disgust, as if no one had even approached his asking price. He pedaled off to another group of soldiers. When he left them, he no longer held the chopper.

At that point, Capt. DeHart came by, tapping me and my M-60, and a dozen other guys for a patrol. We headed to the western end of the airfield, marched into the surrounding jungle and returned along the perimeter of the tarmac. We saw no sign of the enemy.

Returning to our squads and our gear, we spent another nervous night on the ground.

The next morning, the troops were agitated. We sensed that something was going to happen.

"OK, we'll have an Eagle Flight in here to get you clowns," the lieutenant said. He was talking about troop-carrying choppers that would get us into action quickly.

"Get your shit together. Let's not have any horsing around."

I was assigned to a detail that unloaded C-rations from a supply truck. As I worked, I kept an eye to the sky, where a silver Air Force spotter plane was circling.

The plane landed and pulled to a stop in front of a group of officers who were standing around a picnic table covered with maps. The pilot cut the engines and walked to the table. The officers pointed to the hills, the pilot pointed to the maps, they made some calls on their field radios. Then the pilot got back in the plane, buzzed in one direction, did a flip, buzzed in the other direction and, in five minutes, landed in front of the table again. As the engines idled, an officer walked to the cockpit and held up a map.

The pilot nodded and flew off.

I'd finished my chore and stood watching the spotter plane take off and another cargo plane full of Vietnamese land. The C-123 had barely taken off when the sky began filling with helicopters, fifteen to twenty of them.

We grabbed our gear. In the whirlwind and commotion, squad and platoon leaders were waving their arms and screaming above the noise, directing the men who were running for the landing choppers.

Guys were excited as they threw their gear aboard. This was no phony BS., no going from one firebase to another. This was a combat assault we were going on.

Rumor had it we were going almost into Cambodia.

Getting even

Released from the boredom of the past several days, we were ready for action of any kind. There was something else fueling our willingness to fight.

Revenge.

Guys were still outraged by the ransacked village we'd seen passed on the previous week's convoy. Many believed our operation was at least partly in retaliation for the slaughter.

The flock of helicopters cast shadows on the vast green countryside for 10 minutes before landing in a very un-green area. Men who scanned the countryside thought we were being deposited in the bowels of hell.

It was the land of the Arc Light, the site of a bombing strike. The earth was full of holes as large as houses. Dead trees were twisted and wrapped into mounds. The red dirt was blackened and smeared over several hilltops. As the choppers went down, the earth coughed up huge spires of dust.

We had little time to meditate on the scenery. Because we didn't know who or what might be waiting for us, we could only throw ourselves out of the helicopters and into the dirt, pointing our weapons and dashing away from the whap-whap-whapping blades.

The air assault ended successfully and was unopposed. Everyone relaxed. We began looking around the eerie territory. Medford walked up to me holding a three-foot hunk of shrapnel that he'd found. It was difficult to imagine that the heavy metal, melted until it looked organic, had once been a bomb casing. Another metallic hunk had sliced through a tree as if the thick trunk had been clay.

With fourth platoon on point and second walking behind it, Charlie Company headed down the side of the hill toward an area full of vegetation. I had just crossed the edge of the Arc Light's destruction when all hell broke loose in front of me.

F-105s roared in with Gatling guns flashing, chewing up the hillside. Rockets swished down the valley and blasted trees into the air. Napalm burned and crackled.

"Jesus Christ," someone behind me said. "fourth platoon must've really run into some shit."

But, as radio communications confirmed, the 4th hadn't called in the fire mission. That had been the doing of a forward air observer who had seen two Chinese-made trucks driving toward the infantrymen on the same road.

When the planes flew off, we fanned out on either side of the road, with fourth platoon still leading the way. There was no doubt we were in enemy territory.

The North Vietnamese were not only driving up and down the streets, they'd marked them with signs.

Second platoon advanced into the area where the napalm was still smoldering on the ground. Four burning bodies lay in the ashes. Black and still smoking, they smelled like burnt pork. Guys stared as if they'd never seen death up close—which some of us, including me, had not.

There were two more bodies near the trucks.

The first truck had been blown into charred pieces. The other was riddled full of holes but was otherwise intact. Some guys in front of me stopped to look in the back of the second one and were cursing fiercely as I approached. As I walked by, I saw wooden crates stamped with English block letters. I only glimpsed some of the words

"TO THE PEOPLE OF ... FROM THE QUAKER ... UNITED STATES OF AMERICA..."

The boxes were full of chrome-plated socket sets, which the GIs found hard to believe were simply given as a humanitarian gesture to a languishing people. They figured even gooks couldn't eat wrenches.

It was getting late in the day. One of the officers approached Stotka and asked him to take his squad back in the direction we'd come from to guard engineers who were going to blow up the road to keep out enemy vehicles.

I watched from the side of the road as the engineers set their charges, then took off with the other guards when the shout, "Fire in the hole!" echoed in the woods.

There was an explosion. Birds flew, trees shook. We walked back with the engineers to inspect the damage.

Three holes, each the size and roundness of a manhole cover, dotted the road.

The chief engineer shook his head as if to say, "This won't do at all."

They packed in more explosives and cleared the area.

Kaboom! This time, the road was gone.

When my squad rejoined the company, we were told to set up on a hilltop for the night, while the fourth platoon went out on ambush. While I was readying my M-60 to cover the road below, Stotka came up to me.

"I'll see you in the morning. I'm going to go down and pull ambush."

I grinned. So Mr. Gung-ho was going down to see some action with Sgt. White and his fourth platoon boys.

It was quiet as the darkness settled in. Soon after midnight, an explosion woke me and I heard small arms fire. I rolled over, grabbed the M-60 and aimed it into the brush.

"They're coming! They're heading up the hill!" someone next to me half shouted, half whispered.

Our pulses went wild as we lay there, waiting to be overrun.

"Forget it," came the word at last. "Fourth platoon just popped its ambush."

Thank God, I thought. I rolled over and dozed back to sleep, with a passing thought about Stotka. Steve was probably enjoying the hell out of that ... popping claymore mines, throwing grenades ...

Before long, Stotka came running in, shaking with excitement.

"We got 'em, we got 'em," he said. "It was incredible. These dinks came wandering down the road with flashlights, walking right into it! They knew we were there, we knew they were there, but they came on down waving flashlights. So they set the ambush off."

But our people popped the ambush prematurely, Stotka said. Someone, they figured, had survived it. And the existence of survivors meant it wasn't smart to be rummaging around the ambush scene in the dark.

I listened to the story with the proper degree of enthusiasm, but my body cried out for sleep. I rolled over for a few more hours of rest.

Abe's body

At dawn, the company saddled up to move out. Stotka had already left to scout the ambush area with Sgt. White.

Second platoon had just hit the road when, with a drilling tatatatatatat, a machine gun burst sprayed dirt up on either side of me. With the guys around me, I rolled into a bomb crater for cover. In a second, the firing quit. We heard someone screaming in front of us, so we hopped up and walked forward with weapons and brains locked and loaded.

Fourth platoon's point man, whose height and Lincolnesque beard had earned him the nickname Abe, lay dead, all crumpled and flat beside the cab of the crate-filled truck. Stotka was nearby, nursing a bleeding hand. Apparently, there had been four North Vietnamese soldiers caught in the night's ambush. The only officer among them had been killed, the others were wounded.

One of the surviving NVA had taken shelter in the cab of the truck, where, come morning, Abe had surprised him. The wounded soldier had shot the unwary point man in the head, then taken off into the bush. Stotka found the second survivor—or vice-versa, because the enemy suddenly stood and leveled his rifle at the squad leader's chest. Fortunately for Stotka, White was right behind him and shot down the North Vietnamese, whose shot only creased Stotka's hand.

The fourth platoon wanted revenge for Abe's death. They summoned me and their own machine gunner to join the search for the killer. "He's out there somewhere," one of them stated, "We're going to get that little sonofabitch."

Standing 20 feet apart, the other gunner and I opened up with our M-60s, the heavy hitting rounds churning up the vegetation at the side of the road and ripping deep into the jungle. After fewer than 60 rounds, the other gun stopped and I kept up the frontal assault by myself, with Fisher, my assistant gunner, walking behind me. He snapped together the belts of ammunition feeding my gun.

I walked-forward about 40 feet when someone behind me yelled, "OK, hold it!"

When the bullets stopped spraying, five men moved in front of me, nervously prodding the grass and brush with bayonet-bedecked M-16s.

"We got him!" The dead soldier was curled into a fetal position as they grabbed one of his hands and dragged him out to the road.

The young, tan-uniformed NVA soldier had been shot in the abdomen during the ambush and had tried to treat his wounds with a medical kit. He had apparently been killed by the machine gun fire, which had blown away the side of his head.

I cringed at the sight of the grayish-yellow matter oozing onto the road where they dumped the body, about ten feet from Abe's. The other guys emptied the dead NVA's rucksack and were intrigued by his simple supplies, which included a nesting aluminum pot with compartments that contained rice and gravy. As they examined the belongings, I was struck by the fact that we weren't just fighting guerillas. We were fighting an army of soldiers—soldiers with ID cards, uniforms and Chinese-made weapons.

One weapon, a pistol that Stotka had taken from the ambushed officer, was made in Czechoslovakia. The pistol hung on a hand-tooled leather belt that had a starred, silver-plated buckle. Stotka shrugged off warnings that "Charlie Cong's gonna cut off your balls and stuff 'em in your mouth when he captures you with that thing slung around your hips." He was proud of his souvenir. And he was also proud of his wounded hand. He had it wrapped, ceremoniously, and grinningly demanded his Purple Heart.

Stotka spent most of his time with the life-saving veteran, Sgt. White, but he did take a minute to retrieve my helmet. It had fallen off while I was rattling the machine gun through the brush. Once again, I was disappointed to have the heavy sonofabitch back.

The search for the fourth wounded enemy soldier was on. A trail of blood led into the jungle, and I was among those who followed it. Before long Fisher and I were ordered to hunker down beneath a tree and cover a clearing, through which the other men continued the search.

After a few minutes, we began to hear shouting and gunfire. We couldn't see the source of the commotion, which was behind a heavy uphill tree line. At first we ignored it. Then dirt was being sprayed in our faces from gunfire and the shouting got louder.

"Hey, I think they're talking to us," I said to Fisher, just as someone touched me from behind. I spun around to see a guy from the fourth platoon. He had a frantic expression on his face.

"What the hell," Fisher said. "Are we moving out?"

"Goddamnit, they're shooting at you!" yelled the soldier who was yanking on my sleeve.

We made a quick exit out of range of whoever was strafing us. I was grateful the enemy was living up to his reputation for poor marksmanship.

The sniper and the escaped enemy soldier could have been one and the same. At any rate, we never found him. After an hour of searching, we returned to the bullet-riddled truck. Abe's body was now wrapped in his poncho, his boots sticking out of the green fabric. The NVA whose brains had been blasted had been thrown in the back of the truck with the ambushed officer. Their charred companions were still beside the road.

I sat nearby to eat lunch. As I stepped over Abe to trade someone my peaches for their spaghetti, I was strangely unmoved by the death around me. The morbid sights were just more in a series of bizarre things I was learning to live with.

"Cover your lunch," someone hollered. "Here comes the chopper."

A huge, wasp-like Sky Crane hit the area like a hurricane. Built strong enough to lift railroad cars, it had been called in to pick up the Russian truck. The truck would be dropped in Pleiku, where it and the NVA bodies it contained would be displayed as trophies of war. No doubt, pictures of the Quaker-sent socket sets would also be used to weaken support for the religious pacifists who were protesting the war back home.

Unsuccessful at keeping the dust out of my spaghetti sauce, I looked up to see the truck dangling from the chopper like a spider from its web.

Another chopper would be sent for Abe.

Let the Marines do that

We spent a second evening at the top of the nearby hill. It was a quiet one. Stotka returned from the night's patrol with no ambush tales to tell. The next morning we moved out, walking down the road deeper into enemy territory. We continued to pass the road markers of the North Vietnamese, neatly lettered boards that were hammered onto trees.

Around noon, we stopped in a valley filled with 20-foot-high bamboo and elephant grass and dominated by 10 or 15 enormous trees. After the area was scouted, Capt. DeHart decided to establish a position there, one that was bisected by the road. We were told to form a perimeter in the fields to either side.

Crawford, the radioman, stood in the road like a traffic cop, directing men to the right or the left so that a half-circle of men on either side would provide a ring of defense.

I plunged into the grass on the right. I couldn't see anything but the man in front of me. Only the scouts knew where they were going.

Then someone up ahead yelled.

"Get out, get out! Move back!"

I thought it was a joke until the people up front began to panic. They were pushing me.

"What the hell's going on?"

"Just get out, turn around and get the hell out!"

They were shoving like a crowd in a theater where someone had yelled "Fire!" As it turned out, fire was causing the stampede. As I pushed the guy who'd been in back of me, I could hear crackling and feel intense heat as the flames bulldozed us out of the valley.

The crush of men kept me from going back the way I'd come. A group of us found our way back to the road, but the road didn't stop the flames, which kept chasing us.

"Quick, over here, up the river," someone yelled.

I lunged through the acrid smoke toward the waist-deep stream. I splashed into it and, within a few steps, reached the high bank on the opposite side.

Someone reached down to take my weapon. Guys grabbed my arms and hoisted me onto the bank.

Twenty of us sat there and watched the valley burn. Combustion Charlie had lived up to its name again.

We made radio contact with the men who had found safety farther down the stream, past the point where it flowed across the road. We learned that the entire company was safe. We also learned what had caused the fire. Tall grass had been chopped down so that one section of the field could serve as a LZ. When a sufficient clearing had been made, Andy Day threw a smoke grenade onto it to signal an approaching helicopter. The grenade ignited the newly cut mat of dry, dense grass and the fire spread in seconds.

We headed out to regroup with the other troops. As we neared the road, we rounded a curve and came upon some North Vietnamese army hooches. There were no enemy soldiers in sight, but uniforms hung on trees to dry and fresh food sat in pots over cooking fires. The scene set everyone's nerves on edge.

After some hasty snooping at the enemy camp, we continued our trek to the road. When we reached it, we were eyeballs-to-headlights with another Russian-made truck.

The truck was empty. One of the squad sergeants checked under the hood, in the cab and under the chassis for booby traps. Finding none, he slid behind the wheel and somehow got it started.

"All right!" he hollered. "Toss your gear in here."

So we piled guns and packs in the truck bed, hung onto its edges and rode back to the blackened valley.

The CO had not changed his orders about establishing a perimeter. So, when the company was reassembled, we began digging into the ashen earth, which still radiated warmth from the fire. Fallen trees glowed like enormous embers.

We dug for an hour and a half, with artillery rounds sailing high overhead the whole time. An American firebase—I assumed it was the one where I'd guarded the tree-cutting engineers—was having an artillery duel with the NVA unit on the next hill. The enemy troops couldn't lower their guns enough to hit the soot-covered troops bent over shovels in the valley.

Then we got the order: "Let's go."

Normally, we would have been delighted to stop digging and move out. But rumor had it we were going to charge up that hill and take out the dug-in NVA artillery. We were apprehensive, to say the least.

"Let the Marines do that," somebody muttered. "That's what they're for."

"Saddle up and get ready to move out," Stotka said. "Don't take any more gear than you absolutely have to."

We headed down the road, crossed the stream and stopped at the point where we'd found the truck.

"All right, fall out to either side of the road."

As we moved into the trees, a roaring explosion rocked the earth.

KA-BOOM-BAH! "Everybody saddle up," came an order when the reverberations had stopped.

"We're heading back."

We didn't know what was going on. But no one was about to complain about not assaulting hills.

Bone-seeping fear

Turns out, we'd been moved to protect us from danger, not expose us to it. We found a house-sized crater where the truck had been parked. The engineers had blown it apart, apparently to keep it from falling back into enemy hands. In a classic case of overkill, they must have overpacked the vehicle with explosives. The only distinguishable remnant of the truck was its frame, which lay twisted like a burnt pretzel 50 yards from the crater.

We finished digging and settled in for what turned out to be the first night of the monsoon season. As darkness fell, so did the rain. The torrents turned the sooty earth into a black quagmire. They also jellied our nerves.

I sat behind the M-60, the rain beating down on my back. The rim on my bush hat failed to keep my glasses from getting splashed and, in the darkness, I could barely see the barrel of my gun, much less the road I was guarding. I hoped I'd know what to do—and that the guys on either side of me would be awake—when the enemy came.

I knew they would come that night. Fear seeped into my bones with the dampness. Fear of the unknown, fear of death, fear of everything.

We pulled guard four hours on, four hours off. After the first shift, Stotka came by for his turn at the M-60. He tapped me on the shoulder and told me to go to our makeshift tent for some rest.

But I couldn't sleep. My fearful thoughts were as incessant as the leaking of the poncho strung on nylon cord over my head. I lay there, shaking and wondering what I was doing in that goddamn tent. When they come, they were going to run right through there, and what was I going to do? My gun's over there and, hell, we only dug a position for one man. If they start throwing grenades, it'll be all over. This is shitty, this is craziness, and everybody's gonna get killed doing this kind of shit.

The night strangely passed without trouble. The rain crept out as daylight crept in.

In the morning, we took turns standing in front of a fallen tree, drying our uniforms with the heat of the wall-sized ember that the rain had failed to extinguish. I was drying my flip side when George approached.

"The company's going to stay here until about one o'clock, but we're going on an ambush for a few hours."

The lieutenant led the platoon down the road. By the time we reached a second stream, the day had turned hot.

I dipped my helmet into the cold stream, filled it and dumped the water over my head. I filled it again and drank until my belly was bloated. Everybody's spirits were lifted by the sunshine, the water and the bustle of setting up for the ambush. I sensed a sort of Boy Scout camping brotherhood among the guys, despite the lingering fear in my gut.

Chapter 16: Ambush

When hours passed without an ambush, we relaxed. Two guys played poker, slapping cards down between their legs as they sat, talking in whispers. George and Longest were nearby, talking about home, about what they were going to do with their lives. Just before noon, the lieutenant led us back into the area where we'd spent the night. From there, the company started moving again. My squad was on point. As I listened to the commotion of the troops behind me and scanned the charred valley we were leaving, I shared the feeling some of the others had expressed—that the company was some kind of joke. Everywhere we went, we made too much noise, caused too much damage. Just who did we think we were going to sneak up on? Who the hell did we think we were going to kill?

We were moving quickly. Apparently, DeHart had a timetable for the operation and he was trying to stick to it. We only stopped once, briefly, with Longest and Lynch taking over as point men while Stotka and I sat gobbling tropical chocolate bars. I could feel the sugar energy flowing into my sleep-deprived bloodstream. By 2 p.m., the tree-lined dirt road had narrowed so that it would have been touch-and-go to get a truck down it. With my weapon at the ready, I was fourth man back, with Stotka directly in front of me. Lynch and Longest were out ahead, sniffing the air, dodging from side to side, then motioning the rest of us forward.

Lynch and Longest headed around a bend, to the point where I could barely see them. I heard a command shouted in Vietnamese. The voice was followed by the klack-klack-klack of AK-47 fire, then a few M-16 rounds.

I dropped to the ground. Stotka, in the dirt beside me, ordered me to open fire. I started to obey, pointing my M-60 toward the noises. But as my finger touched the trigger, I saw Longest high-tail it through the underbrush in the direction I was aiming. I let go of the trigger as Lynch backed out of the bush in front of me.

"You take over point," Stotka said to Lynch. "C'mon, Hoss."
I rolled out of my pack, leaving it on the ground, and followed Stotka. He was sprinting.

"What are you doing?" I asked, breathlessly.
"We're chasing that little motherfucker!"

We were well ahead of the others when Stotka saw movement among the trees. "There he is! There's that little gook sonofabitch!"

We took few more steps down the trail when bullets ripped past our ears and two loud klacks of rifle fire sounded over our heads. "We'll get that little fucker yet!"

"Steve, what th..!" I said as we kept running. I couldn't understand why we were wasting so much time chasing one soldier when, for all we knew, a whole enemy battalion was attacking Charlie Company. What good was my machine gun way the fuck out here? We were following black flat communication wire that ran along the side of the road. It was becoming obvious that the enemy soldier we were chasing was a lone scout.

"Hey," I protested. "We oughta be getting back."

Stotka slowed his pace. The woods were quiet. We were a long way from the squad.

"Yeah, I guess we'll never find the little fucker out here," he said in a less boisterous voice. Then he shifted his eyes, which had been scanning the trees, to look at me.

"Why didn't you open fire when you were back there?" he demanded.

"Because I'd hit my own people, that's why."

"Goddamnit, you're supposed to open fire. When I say open fire, I mean open fire."

"Well, goddamnit, the other guys were still out in front of us. You know that."

Stotka turned and I followed. We rejoined Lynch, Longest and the other squad members who had made their way to the front during the few minutes we'd been gone. A patrol was sent ahead along the trail to cut the commo line.

As the four of us headed out in front of the column again, Stotka was subdued. I sensed that he was still angry over my not shooting. But, damn it, I wasn't going to spray lead when my buddies were in the line of fire.

About 16:00 hours, we stopped at a shallow river. The lieutenant and captain moved up to survey the area with their binoculars, then called in a reconnaissance plane.

Within 15 minutes, the company started crossing the river. Although second platoon waded across first, I was the last one to get my feet wet, because I had to stay behind with my weapon to cover the fording.

M-60 held high, I finally stepped into the cool water and crossed to the other bank. As I walked into the woods, I tried to shake the mud and weeds from my boots.

George, who was waiting to lead me up to the point position, laughed.

"God, Hoss, you walk like an old woman with the crabs!" he said, giving me a good-hearted shove toward the front.

Shit, that's a helluva thing to say, I thought. Sorry I can't walk to your satisfaction.

As I passed through the ranks, one of the guys pointed to the ground.

"What the hell is that?" he asked, more to confirm the existence than the identity of the object that held his attention.

"It's a Chi-com grenade!"

"That's what I thought."

"Well, don't step..."

"OK."

The glistening green grenade was a sure sign of enemy in the vicinity, but we were more concerned for the moment about disposing of it than we were about flushing out its owners. I walked on as one of guys gingerly tossed it behind us in the river.

When I reached the front, I was assigned an assistant machine gunner, a blond soldier named Ken Hesson. The two of us joined Stotka, Lynch and Longest and traveled silently for about five minutes before those three spotted something. They dashed to one side of the trail. Stotka looked back, his wide eyes seeking me out.

"C'mon, get out of your gear," he whispered.

I shrugged out of my pack.

"Goddamnit, there they go!" Stotka said loudly. "Go get them!"

I saw three tan figures scamper off the trail and start diving ahead to the left. I fired a long burst. My eyes squinted following my sight line to three twisting figures falling awkwardly into the churning brush.

My God, I thought. I've actually killed those people.

"Go check 'em, go check 'em, keep going," Stotka called out, his voice a blend of excitement and anxiety.

Firing from the hip, I walked forward. Just when I could see the soles of the dead enemy's sandals, I heard a hollow da-dunt sound from my weapon's chamber, followed by a loud silence. The M-60 had run out of ammo, and I had only one bandolier remaining around my chest. My heart raced. My ammo-filled pack, and my assistant's, seemed much further than a few yards away.

"Get back!" Stotka yelled. I didn't hesitate to follow the order. But as I turned, bullets started zipping past my head. I dashed back to the spot in the middle of the road where I'd left my pack. As I grabbed for it, I heard Stotka squeal and saw the second of two rounds go into his back. The squad leader fell into the road, then picked himself up and ran to the rear, screaming and shaking his head violently. On the other side of me, another soldier screamed, then crawled into the brush after his body had been slammed into the road.

Lynch and Longest were stalking behind the trees, firing at unseen enemy. They were reacting to the ambush as they'd been taught—by taking the offensive.[4]

Green tracers splattered into the dirt around us. Hesson rushed up beside me and started linking a couple of belts of ammo together. Down on one knee, I opened the feed tray hatch, lay the rounds into position. As I slammed the hatch down, it snagged on the gun's sling. Frantically, I slammed it again and it caught on the fabric again. In my anxiety to get the gun loaded, I ripped the sling off the front of the barrel and threw it back to dangle behind me. Now I got it locked and loaded. Pivoting on my knee, I turned and fired, using up ammunition as fast as Hesson could slap ammo belts together.

---

[4] The combatants included Don Newton and Warren Niederfringer. Squad member Bob Robbins recalls that, when he saw the duo moving forward and firing, "my respect for them increased tremendously. They were real troopers."

Then the ambush opened up. Grenades went off on either side of us, throwing dirt and vegetation into the air. Hundreds and hundreds of green tracer rifle rounds zipped down.

God, or no God

"They're in the trees!"

The words were barely out of my mouth when I was hit. It felt as if someone had welded a 10-penny nail to a sledgehammer and slammed it into my left shoulder.

The frenzied fighting screeched into slow motion. It seemed to take 15 minutes for my M-60 to drop, 30 minutes for me to fall backward. With a lingering, sonic-level boom, a grenade exploded beside me and threw my body up and over to one side. My head thudded down and my eyes, which had been focusing on the leaves that shimmered and shook in the sunlight above me, began to roll back in their sockets.

They finally did it, I thought, they finally killed me. Then, through the numbness that seized me, a notion crept in. Maybe I should acknowledge that there is a God, I thought. With a sense of relief, I dismissed the idea—having once put much energy into concluding that there is no all-powerful, judgmental being—and replaced it with another thought: Now I would find out what death is like.

Lying in the middle of the road, I became aware of Hesson kneeling over me. He was staring down aghast, as if I had personally affronted him by daring to be shot.

Hesson picked the M-60 off my lap and started firing. Through the ammo links that were rattling into my face, I could see his back. Three red spots suddenly appeared there, spreading like ink stains in the olive shirt. Hesson gasped and fell onto me, burning my left forearm with the machine gun's hot barrel.

The burn, Hesson's weight and even the bullet wound were not causing me as much agony as my helmet, which was lodged under my neck. I'd been thrown on it by the grenade blast, after a rifle round had grazed its top and lifted it off my head.

At least I was alive. So was Hesson, who was gasping and groaning. But not George. From the corner of my eye, I could see the lieutenant's body lying a few feet away with two bloody circles on his back. As far as I knew, his last words were "God, Hoss, you walk like an old lady with the crabs."

Twice George's distance from me, and out of my sight, was a fat soldier who had been playing cards that morning. He was badly wounded, and I was tormented by his screams until they turned to guttural gurgling. He was drowning in his own blood.

Among the screams, I heard frantic shouted commands. Some came from the Vietnamese. I glimpsed their feet as they ran past, not 10 feet from my head. Lynch was still intact and, when a grenade went off in front of him, he dashed to the rear. Longest was then the only man in the vicinity who was capable of firing back at the enemy, and he was mad with fear. He pressed up against a tree for cover and was repelled by a grenade or rifle fire each time he tried to move. It was forever—maybe five minutes after I'd been shot—before I heard someone screaming from the rear.

"Move back, get back here, get back. If you can make it, come back!"

I couldn't retreat. I could barely move my arms or legs. But Hesson didn't seem to be paralyzed.

"Are you all right?" I asked him. "Can you make it back?"

"Yeah, I think I can make it," Hesson groaned. As he rolled off and crawled away, bullets spat at the dirt all around him.

When Longest saw Hesson make it to the rear, he apparently decided that it was time for him to get out, too. As he left the shelter of the tree and started running, a grenade was thrown in front of him. Blood splattered as the explosion peeled back his face. He screamed through hands that clutched his mangled features and ran another five feet before he was shot in the back. I watched as Longest arched forward, hitting the ground with his legs bent at the knees and his feet pointing into the air. But he kept moving, crawling at first and then jumping onto his feet and sprinting toward safety.

As far as I could tell, I was the last breathing American left in the open. I heard sporadic firing. M-79 rounds arched over my head, booming behind me. I grimaced, afraid that one of the grenades would fall short and land on me. Occasionally, something or someone would brush my feet.

I assumed that the enemy assumed I was dead. When they found out otherwise, the best I could hope for was to take some of them with me or to kill myself to keep them from dragging me off and torturing my ass. So I concentrated on using what little movement I had on an effort to reach my pistol.

But I was stymied by the cheap holster that I'd inherited with the .45. The holster, which had no way of fastening to one spot on a leather belt, had slid around to my back. I was directly on top of it and found it painfully impossible to reach. I gave up when I realized there was no way I could load and cock the pistol, which I kept empty because of its dangerous habit of cocking as it caught on brush.

As I waited and listened to the screams of a wounded Vietnamese, a helicopter appeared in the patch of sky that broke through the tall trees above my head. The small, hornet-like Loach chopper, with its mini-guns, was moving in a tight circle.

I was relieved, especially when I saw Hawk's long scarf dangle as the pilot stuck his head out the window. The cavalry had arrived.

Then I could hear the NVA on either side of me loading and locking the big banana clips on the AKs. They started rattling rounds at the helicopter, chunks of which began falling from the sky. Hawk zipped his head in and flew off. I laughed out loud as I heard the mini-guns open up on some other target. It was absurd. There I was, needing to be rescued, and Hawk was so afraid that he probably went off and shot a water buffalo.

I didn't laugh long. The pain was getting severe, and I didn't want to make any more noise for fear of drawing fire. I managed to take off my glasses and began gnawing on the earpieces to keep my mind off the pain.

As five or 10 Vietnamese soldiers moved past me, I heard voices calling my name.

"Hoss, are you all right? Can you get up and outta there?"

If I answered, I'd be shot again. If I didn't, they'd leave me behind. It wasn't that the Army wouldn't be back to retrieve my carcass; I just figured that I'd bleed to death before the Americans could counterattack.

As I agonized and listened to their voices, rounds kept going off around me.

There was not going to be a lull in the fighting.

"Come back if you're out there, Hoss, and you can hear us. Come on back. Are you out there? Can you talk? We'll come and get you. Say something. Are you out there?"

"Yes, goddamnit, I'm out here!"

The enemy soldier who fired this time could have been no more than 10 feet away. Two bullets hit my right leg and flipped me onto my left side. The impact knocked me off my helmet—a welcome but minor improvement to my situation. Just as my body came to rest, an enemy grenade hit the ground near me and rolled a few feet away, only to fizzle out.

I was, again, surprised to be alive. I resolved not to say another word.

Coming for me

The sounds of bullets, grenades and screaming soldiers increased incredibly. The Vietnamese were retreating, dragging their wounded with them but never letting up on their small arms barrage.

With my head tilted back and to one side, I could see someone crawling toward me.

It was the company's myopic medic, the one who had treated me for heat exhaustion and who always had eight extra pairs of glasses hanging from his belt. Fear radiated from behind his thick lenses. As bullets kicked up dirt around him, his olive skin turned pale and poured with sweat.

"Boy, am I glad to see you," I said through teeth gritted with pain.

The shaking medic bellied up to me.

"Where ya hit? Where ya hit?" he yelled over the gunfire.

"I don't know."

My shoulder hurt, but most of the pain was in my upper back. My whole body was covered with blood, much of it Hesson's.

Laying himself over me to keep below the strafing, the medic got out a knife and cut my upper left sleeve. Seeing only a neat hole in the shoulder, he moved down to tend my wounded leg.

The flesh had been blown inside out just below my knee. The sight of it and, probably, his own wrenching fear caused the medic to gag. He recovered quickly, bandaging the wound and wrapping a tourniquet above it. He also put a bandage over a lesser wound in the thigh, but didn't mess with the shoulder.

The pain was outpacing my ability to suppress it.

"I know you give one Syrette of morphine, but I could sure use two," I said. "I'm a big boy."

"Yeah," the medic replied. He injected the morphine into my neck, then stuck the empty little tubes into my lapel it to indicate how much he'd given me.

"Where's your pack?" the medic yelled as he stuffed away his supplies. He lowered his ear to my mouth so he could hear my answer over the battle sounds.

"I don't know. It's around here somewhere."

The medic, still keeping low, found a pack nearby and ripped out a rubberized poncho. He spread it beside me.

"Can you roll over on that?"

"I don't know."

He grabbed my bad arm and rolled me stomach-down onto the poncho.

"Just wait here a minute," the medic said, as if I had a real choice in the matter.

The Americans who'd been laying down a protective barrage as the medic worked kept up their fire as he crawled back to them.

Now what?

Then they came for me, six GIs running and firing from the hip. One guy toted two M-16s; another was throwing grenades. They barely broke their stride as those with free hands grabbed the poncho and dragged me out of the road.

It was just like the movies. Some part of me grinned.

The firing continued as the rest of the company charged past in the other direction. As soon as my rescuers deposited me in a clearing, they turned around to join the counteroffensive.

The medic returned to bandage my arm, rewrap my leg wounds and tear open my bloody shirt to look for more damage. Then he moved on to another wounded man who was lying a couple of yards to the left. To my right was George's body.

George's death had devastated the radio operator, who had been his friend, assistant and roommate for nearly a month. I could hear the big RTO crying like a kid into the phone as he called in air strikes. His sobs were more easily understood than his directions. George was dead. The lieutenant was gone.[5]

The medic returned to me. He crouched down, lit a cigarette in his own mouth, lifted my head and transferred the smoke to my lips before gently lowering my head to the ground.

I didn't want the cigarette and didn't need the nicotine to calm my nerves. The morphine was taking hold. My body grew numb as I looked up to see the troops regrouping after the 10-minute counterattack.

They stared back at me, at George, at the other wounded and dead. Their eyes were bloodshot, their skin was white. Some were shaking. Their silence as intense, like they were in a funeral procession. We'd always joked about a wound being a ticket home, but no one said "God, Hoss, you've got it made."

Lynch walked by, carrying the M-60. He had sworn time and again that he would "never carry that goddamn thing because it weighs too much and is such a hassle."

---

[5] According to Bob Robbins, the radio operator who so mourned the loss of Lt. George Callan was Dennis Harris.

I thought it poetic justice that the Southerner should end up with it. All you had to do was touch the pig and it was yours.

They were still filing past when two helicopter crewmen transferred me to a stretcher and carried me away. I lost consciousness as the chopper rose into the air.

Chapter 17: Travelogue of the wounded

I was plied with painkillers during the following weeks of hospital-hopping. Those days in March 1969 were as blurred as the chopper blades that lifted me from red dirt to white sheets.

We'd landed near a field hospital—at Dak To?—and the good-natured gripes of the orderlies who lugged my stretcher caused me to raise my heavy eyelids. "God, what a big S.O.B."

I was a shadow of my pre-Army self, but still big enough to intimidate anyone who had to carry me.

They lifted me off the stretcher and put me on a table. I was aware of the lights and of the bodies around me, maybe 10 of them on similar metal slabs.

Medical teams of three or four hovered over each of us. It was a methodically frantic place.

A doctor gave me the once-over, decided I was not in immediate danger of dying, and put me in the charge of a nurse. She was a blonde and, as well as I could discern through my sedated mind and her fatigues, quite attractive. My eyes followed her as she cut into the webbing of my jungle boots. As other hands pulled off the boots, she clipped at my shirt with blunt scissors. She was about to start on my pants when her shift ended.

As the evening crew came on, another nurse took up where her friend had left off. The nurses exchanged gossip for a moment before the first one parted with a lilting "G'night."

Soon I was lying naked under the bright fluorescent lights. The doctor came back. He prodded and poked gently, checking every square inch of me as the nurse made notations on a chart. Then I was lifted onto a gurney, covered with a light blanket and rolled to the X-ray room.

I was lifted again and strapped loosely to another table, which was then tilted forward. A dark-haired, lab-coated character began to examine my wounded arm. He saw only a bullet hole in the middle of a large bruise.

"Lift your arm," he said.

"I can't."

"Well, let me have a look at it." As he spoke, he reached for the arm and began to move it up and down at the shoulder. I screamed.

"You goddamn fucking sonofabitch, stop screwing ..."

Then I passed out from the worst pain of my life.

I woke up four hours later in a dim, four-bed ward. Twilight was visible through a single wire-meshed window.

They had cleaned my wounds. My right leg was in a cast. There was a bandage below the shoulder socket that, the X-rays had shown, was blown half away by the bullet that entered my arm. Repair work on both limbs would have to wait for other surgeons.

From my bed against the outer wall, I could see nurses bustling at the hallway station. The patient in the next bed had a bandaged hand and introduced himself quietly as an Air Force major. On the other side of the room, in the third bed, was a sleeping soldier whose chest and upper face were bandaged. A familiar goatee protruded below the facial wrapping and the dogtags on top of the chest dressing were strung with love beads. I grinned at the sight. Longest had made it.

The fourth bed was occupied by a guy with a long nose, olive skin, beard and dark, wavy hair that was long enough to cover his ears. He certainly didn't look military.

The long-nosed man, who was sitting up and reading under a bed light, looked back at me and smiled. When he put down his book and swung his feet to the floor, I could see that he wore a black shirt with a clerical collar. It was impossible to tell what bandages were hidden by the shirt and pants, but his walk was painfully slow as he crossed the room.

The religious man touched my forehead, held my hand and said something in French. For the next 15 minutes he sat beside the bed, speaking occasionally but communicating mostly through the concern in his eyes.

When the priest had blessed me and returned to his bed, the major propped himself on one elbow and told me about the Frenchman. He was the only survivor of the Montagnard village massacre that had enraged Company C. Bayoneted and left for dead, he had rolled beneath one of the stilted buildings. He had lost consciousness while the North Vietnamese slaughtered the orphans who were his students.

And the major himself? He had ripped a finger off his hand as he jumped out of the C-47 he had just landed. His wedding ring caught on a protuberance from the gunship's hatch. It was a seven- or eight-foot drop.

When the major's stories were over, I noticed that Longest was awake.

"Hey, Brent, that's you, isn't it?"

"Hoss? How the hell are ya?" he asked, turning his bandaged eyes in the direction of my voice.

"They hit me in the shoulder and leg. I'll live."

We didn't talk for long. It wasn't clear to me if Longest would get his vision back. What I did know was that my own pain was returning. I was grateful to see the nurse who came in with a syringe full of relief, something that let me sleep through the night.

When the next morning's breakfast trays had been cleared, a hefty master sergeant appeared at the door, pushing a typewriter cart. It squeaked across the floor as he rolled it to my bedside. He sat down at the typewriter, fed it some paper and looked over at me.

"Well," he asked. "What happened?"

The sergeant took notes as I recounted the circumstances of the ambush.

Satisfied, he wheeled his typewriter over to Longest.

A lieutenant came in. He seemed ill at ease, as if the occasion called for a bit of ceremony that he couldn't quite muster. He walked up to me opened a small black case and displayed the Purple Heart within it. He closed the case, set it on the nightstand and handed me a copy of orders that qualified me for the honor. After the lieutenant expressed the country's gratitude, he walked to Longest's bed and repeated the presentation.

My morning shot of Demerol was taking effect and I fell asleep as the sergeant squeak, squeak, squeaked his way out of the room.

When I woke up, I had more company. It was Stork and several other officers, come to see the curiosities of the lieutenant's last command. I gave them a sketchy report of the previous day's combat.

The next visitor was Stotka, who hobbled in on crutches and eased himself into the bedside chair to talk for awhile. He filled me and Longest in on the names of the wounded and the extent of the counteroffensive. But the words sunk into my narcotic haze like so many rocks. The most memorable part of the conversation was Stotka's undampened enthusiasm and his hopes for further glory.

"God, Hoss, I hear they're thinking about giving us Silver Stars."

"What the fuck for? Forget it, Steve. We didn't do anything above and beyond the call of duty—we just did our fucking jobs. And maybe we didn't do 'em that well. Forget the Silver Star."

Stotka didn't receive the advice with a great deal of enthusiasm. Before long, he said good-bye and hobbled out of my life.

The next day, I was flown to the Army hospital at Cam Ranh Bay. It was a huge, Quonset-shaped building that was packed with wounded, like a scene from a Civil War movie.

Two days later, I was bused to the nearby Air Force hospital. It was modern, low-ceilinged and spread out. Wards jutted in every direction like the legs of a spider. It was there, when the lights were lowered for the night and the bustling was subdued, that I heard some most amazing stories.

Of the 20 men in my ward, half a dozen swapped tales of their exploits. Part brag, part confession, each story led to another. Many of them dealt with abuse, the kind I expected to hear linked with the enemy.

A lieutenant from the American Division talked about joining forces with the Koreans to check out a village where a suspected informer lived. Something—maybe a radio part found in her hooch—led the allies to believe that an old woman was collaborating with the Viet Cong. They interrogated her, to no avail. Then the lieutenant watched as the Koreans killed her. They pulled down her pants, rammed a rocket flare up her vagina, and popped it.

The private in the bed next to me was a truck driver who told with relish of how he ran over Vietnamese. He would wait until one of them was behind him riding a moped. When a cyclist got close enough to be accused of tailgating, the driver would slam on his brakes. And what a blast it was when a hut got in the way of his vehicle.

A land mine under the truck bed put an end to the driver's fun.

Not all the stories were gruesome. One of my favorites was shared by Morrow, one of my basic training buddies. I'd spotted Morrow, who was in the 1st Air Cavalry Division, pulling himself on crutches through the ward. He told me that he arrived at his first firebase assignment only to have the company pack into helicopters and fly away while he and another replacement continued to stand O.P. for no one. It was a full, fearful day after they were abandoned before they frantically flagged down a passing Huey. The suspicious gunship pilot circled for a long time and called in another Huey before a third chopper was summoned to rescue the stranded soldiers.

Winter air

The next day, I was moved again, this time to Japan via a C-141. Medford was on the flight, too. From his rack across the aisle, he filled me in on the extent of his leg wounds and what he could recall of the ambush. We spoke off and on until the transport landed in Tokyo.

The helicopter ride from the airport to the 249th General Hospital in Asaka was exhilarating. My position on the middle rack permitted a tourist's view of the city through the window. As I was lifted on and off, the wintry air hit my lungs like cold water after three months of breathing hot, humid Vietnam.

When I was settled into my hospital bed, a nurse brought me a phone and helped put through a call to Idaho. A drowsy voice answered.

"Hello."

"Hi, Mom. It's me, Grady. Now don't get worried, but I've been shot. I'm in Japan."

"Are you sure? Are you sure you're all right?" Her voice was worried with a capital W. She turned away from the receiver. "Zeke, Zeke, Grady's been shot!" I could picture her in the light of her bedside lamp.

"Hello, Son?"

"Yeah, Dad."

"How bad are you hurt?"

"Just bad enough to come home, that's all. I was hit in the shoulder and leg. Machine gun fire. I'm in Tokyo."

There wasn't much more to the call. It ended with my promise to write with details. My latest dose of sedative took hold as the overseas operator broke the connection.

I was back out in the cold air the next day, when I had to leave the ward for the X-ray room in another building. I was accompanied by a patient who not only volunteered to push my wheelchair, but seemed to have adopted me.

The volunteer was a Marine of Italian extraction. He was vibrant, happy as only a survivor can be. In his second week overseas, he had taken part in a battle in Cambodia in which all the other men in his company had been killed. The single bullet that found him had broken his arm. He was being sent home. As he talked boisterously and gestured grandly with his free arm, he obviously was pleased to be alive. So very pleased.

The Marine hung around the X-ray room with me, his voice ringing out above the squalling babies and talking mothers among the military dependents.

When the X-rays had been taken, we headed back to the ward.

On the way, the Marine stopped the wheelchair in front of a door that was slightly open.

"Hey, this is where they keep the basket cases. Let's take a look."

The room was darkened by pulled shades. There were various kinds of beds filled with bodies—or what was left of them—in sometimes-strange positions. It was an oddly quiet world of fluid-filled tubes and attached bags full of ... We didn't look close enough to find out, but turned and left within a minute.

Although the most grotesquely injured soldiers were separated from the rest, death was no stranger to the other wards. Four times during my stay in Tokyo, something—a death rattle?—woke me during the night. One corner of the ward would come alive. Lights were flipped on, curtains were pulled, orders were given and sometimes, in a vain attempt at resuscitation, the dying man's chest was pounded. Then the orders stopped.

A gurney was wheeled in. After it rolled out with its sheet-covered burden, the ward was quiet again.

Despite the death and pain, the hospital wasn't depressing. Besides displaying genuine concern, the medical personnel cheerfully accepted the eccentricities of their charges. They accepted the fact that soldiers aren't likely to be model patients. A man just off the battlefield, though accustomed to following orders, is also used to certain independence. He is certainly not used to coddling. After sleeping in a foxhole, just being ensconced in a bed seems an outrageous luxury.

One thing that set the soldiers apart as patients was black humor. Wounds and death were the most common subject of jokes. Nothing quite caused the guys to split their stitches laughing as the violence they watched on the ward televisions. The Japanese programs were not for the squeamish. A Palladin-like character who slashed the bad guys in half with a swoop of his sword was a favorite of the bedridden viewers.

Some of the men with the least to laugh about were the most cheerful. Among them were two guys who were beside me in the second ward I occupied at the 249th. Both were covered with casts, except for their heads and one arm each.

The one with a free right arm was a 30-ish Army major who looked like the British comedian Terry-Thomas, right down to the space between his front teeth. The major's body had been shattered, but miraculously not punctured, by a mine that exploded under his jeep and killed two other passengers.

The one with a free left arm was a sergeant, young for his rank because he had lied to the Army about his age and enlisted at 16. On his third tour in Vietnam, he'd stood at the door of the helicopter when his company had lifted off a hot landing zone, pumping rounds at the enemy who were overrunning the LZ. The next thing he knew, he was in a hospital. He'd been rescued after falling a couple of hundred feet.

The immobile soldiers, who weren't fit to be shipped anywhere, became close friends in their months at the hospital. Each had a long piece of bamboo that he could use to reach inside his cast or, when he wasn't relieving himself of an itch, could use to beat his buddy. The two had a hundred private jokes and I felt that my presence might be intruding on their friendship.

For the most part, I was too drugged to contemplate anything. Such was the case during my return trip to the U.S. Except for the cold Japanese air and the throbbing of engines on the windowless C-141, I felt very little.

I was somewhat clear-headed as I settled in for a night at the Travis Air Force Base hospital near Fairfield, Calif. I was put next to Morrow, the training buddy I'd last seen in Cam Ranh Bay.

"Are you fuckers hungry?" asked the first orderly to check our charts.

"What's on the menu?"

"Steak and eggs. Everybody comin' in gets steak and eggs."

When we'd polished off the last of the eggs, Morrow started to talk. He wanted to discuss his wound. He had been shot in the groin and wasn't sure of his sexual future. How was his fiancée going to take the news? This was the first time I'd known someone who suffered that type of injury, although it was a constant topic of conversation in the infantry. I didn't know what to say. I could only express concern— "Damn, that's a shit-eating deal"—and try not to listen when Morrow huddled over the telephone on his bed and tearfully told his girl that he might not be up to his manly duties.

My cast was getting rank from the constant drainage of my leg wounds. My injuries needed much more attention before they could begin to heal and my steadfast refusal to use a bedpan made them worse. In the overseas hospitals, where I'd been too weak to lift myself, I demanded to be helped to the toilet. At Travis, I used my moveable arm and leg to work my way to the edge of the bed, lower the heavy cast to the floor and hobble to the john. The effort forced blood and pus out of the gaping hole in my thigh.

It was more than disdain for bedpans that motivated these painful maneuvers. It was my need for a show of independence. I figured that there was still, by God, one thing in my life over which I had more control than the Army.

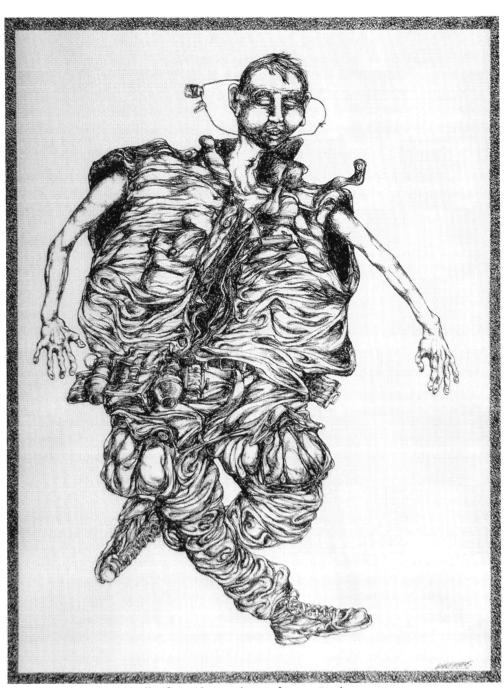
Still Life with Combat Infantry Badge

Chapter 18: Fitzsimmons

I was shot on March 5, 1969. On March 17, I was eating pizza in a hallway of Fitzsimmons General Army Hospital in Denver.

The bus full of chattering, cane-rattling casualties—all pleased to be reaching a secure and reasonably permanent destination—had been driven through an evening drizzle from the airport. During the hubbub of unloading the wounded, I was placed on a gurney, covered with a white blanket and pushed to one side of the marbled central hall.

The hustle and bustle was over as quickly as it had begun and I found myself alone. There was nary a patient or an orderly in sight when a group of hospital volunteers walked by, breaking the silence with their chatting.

One of them, a middle-aged woman, stopped to look down at me.

"Hi. Did you just get in?"

"Yeah."

"Well, here. Have a pizza," she said, placing a flat box on my chest and smiling. "Sorry it's not all there."

As my benefactor departed, I raised my head and peered into the box. Half a large pepperoni. It was cold, but munching on it kept me occupied for the next hour. About the time I decided I'd been forgotten, someone wordlessly pushed me to the X-ray department.

By the time I settled into bed, my ward was well into the throes of Beer Night.

Beer Night came each Friday, when an orderly wheeled around a silver trash can full of ice and Hamms, and dispensed one can to each patient. Not that a beer lover couldn't wrangle a second brew. It wasn't long before I learned that, if I faked taking part of my nightly dose of Darvon, I could swap the pills with patients who preferred drugs to alcohol.

For the first few days, until the doctors learned to prescribe large enough doses, I gladly took any narcotics I could get. I hurt most of the time.

A nurse came in twice each day to suction the green puss out of the hole in my thigh. It was weeks before that wound started to heal. Meanwhile, the doctors concentrated on my wounded shoulder. Although the bullet had missed the arteries and major nerves, it had fractured the bone and torn the muscle. Without surgery, my arm would be useless.

I had assumed that the offending bullet, like the ones that hit my leg, had found its way into the red Vietnamese dirt after doing its damage. Not so. I was amazed to discover the bullet under the skin of my neck, where it had worked its way after bypassing my spinal column. The doctors decided to leave it alone and it eventually moved down into my back.

My primary doc was a civilian, one of the many surgeons who made Fitzsimmons the Army's orthopedic treatment center—a made-to-order laboratory for perfecting treatment of shattered limbs. As he explained it, there were three surgical options for my shoulder joint. It could be fused, which would make the arm immobile; it could be replaced with a stainless steel, Teflon-coated joint; or it could be secured with three metallic fasteners, called Steinmann pins. I chose the third option.

"Good," said the doctor. "You'll have pain and it'll get worse as you get older. But at least you'll have some arm movement. I'd hate to have you get that stainless steel joint, then we'd have to go in five years down the road, take it out and put something else in. There's always that possibility."

My mother was included in this discussion. She'd arrived in Denver five days after me, checking into a motel across from the hospital. I woke up one morning to find her auburn-framed face smiling down at me.

The first thing she did was trim my moustache. I did not want to be mothered. It was embarrassing to be fussed over in a roomful of other soldiers. But the weeklong visit seemed to help her. We both liked talking, especially when she helped me into a long, old-fashioned wicker wheelchair and sat with me on the sun deck, both of us bundled against the cool spring air. When she left for home, her eyes were less puffy and red.

Surgery was scheduled for March 26. The night before, a nurse shaved the left half of my chest in preparation for the scalpel. The shaving was a simple procedure, but not easy for her. She was a young, plump Mormon. She looked so much like the Pillsbury Dough Boy that I was tempted to poke her in the belly and watch her giggle.

When she came into the ward, the patients who could get out of bed surrounded her like vultures. They knew what she was going to do and, it being Beer Night, proceeded to give her a hard time.

"You're gonna hafta get real close to him, honey."

"Be careful when you cut around that nipple!"

She was shaking by the time she reached my bed. I eyed the tray she was carrying. It contained a towel, pHisoHex and a disposable razor. A disposable straight razor.

"No way are you going to get near me with that goddamned thing!" I told her.

Which led to another round of catcalls from the men, who were at the nurse's elbow, jostling her and having a great time. I told them to knock it off.

The nurse left the room with tears on her round cheeks.

"God, you guys scared her away for good. Now you're gonna be in goddamn trouble."

Fifteen minutes later, she returned with a safety razor and went to work. This time, the men were quieter and edged back ever so slowly to watch her scrape off the soap and curly red chest hairs.

They gasped in unison as her razor approached my nipple. Her eyes got misty and she started to shake again, but she finished the job without a nick. Then she dashed off, toting her little tray.

Pieced back together

I went into surgery in early morning and woke in late afternoon. Rows of metal sutures—maybe 120 of them—bound the overlapping flaps of shoulder flesh that had been peeled back by the surgeon.

The sutures got caught on the sheets for several weeks until the nurse came to take them out. By that time, my arm had atrophied until it could have belonged to a flesh-covered skeleton. The surgical wound looped around my shoulder like a braided citation lanyard.

I would lie for hours in bed, concentrating on moving my arm. For six weeks, nothing happened. Then, one morning, I budged it from my upper chest down to my navel. I was exhausted by the effort, but so relieved that I cried.

One month to the day since I'd been shot, I regained enough strength to walk. With the help of a walking cast, a crutch and my 18-year-old brother, Ken, I maneuvered along the sidewalk in front of the hospital.

The first two months on the ward passed quickly. My pain was ebbing and there was always someone around with an interesting story to tell.

The curly haired patient in the bed to one side of me had been caught out in the snow in Germany and had suffered frostbite. Once I was teasing him and lifted the flap on the tent-like covering above his damaged feet. They looked like black logs with chunks on them. I tweaked one of the chunks—a toe—and it fell off. I was floored. The guy didn't feel a thing.

For awhile, the bed on the other side was also occupied by someone with frostbitten feet. Only his injury had been acquired in the mountains of Colorado, where he headed after going AWOL. He turned himself into the Army in order to get free medical care. He was a happy-go-lucky sort and I liked him even though he stole the earplugs from the radio my mom brought me.

The Army treated the AWOL character well, all things considered. They gave him a less-than-honorable discharge, but never sent him to jail. The hospital staff even tolerated his beard and long hair.

One thing that wasn't tolerated, at least by the other patients, was any man who whined. One of the few who bitched and moaned about his fate had lost his legs. I heard he'd been monkeying around with a .50-caliber and had shot himself with his own machine gun.

The other men told him to "Lay off the goddamn crying and be a man." When he didn't, they gave him a hard time. Sometimes, when he grabbed the bar above his bed and swung himself out to plop down in his wheelchair, the chair would be missing. The ward went wild with laughter as he hung there, flailing his stumps and bellowing for an orderly to come and help him.

There was little the staff could do but chide the offenders. How could you discipline a soldier if you couldn't give him KP, throw him in the brig or make him stand extra guard duty?

Rank still had its privileges in the hospital. While the enlisted men were carousing in the wards, the wounded officers were sometimes carrying on in their private rooms. One captain fell in love with the Pillsbury nurse, who spent an inordinate amount of time tending to his wounds.

In early May, I was transferred to one of the two-story brick barracks that surrounded the main hospital. There were eighty or ninety men there, a raucous bunch watched over by a few orderlies. We were roused each morning, just like in the regular Army, and fell into a routine of treatment and physical therapy.

The only bright spot in the dull routine was an attractive physical therapist. She was a captain with short, dark hair and tight, crisp uniforms. It made the patients hornier than hell to have her leaning over them saying, "Oh, you can push harder than that!"

What made the captain even sexier was our knowing she was not above fraternization. She was having an affair with one of my new buddies, a mustachioed sergeant named Jerry whose lower right leg was missing but whose libido was definitely intact.

I left for a two-week leave full of beer drinking and storytelling in Boise. When people caught sight of me on crutches, with civilian pants slit to cover my long white leg cast, they asked if I'd got hurt up at Bogus Basin. I guess I did look like someone who'd whacked himself on the ski hill. I didn't advertise my military status. But at night, when the lights in the family split-level were turned off, I felt uneasy sleeping without a weapon. So I got out an old single-action Colt pistol that I'd bought before I went overseas. It had its original holster, bought new through Sears and Roebuck in 1906, and I slung that on my bedpost.

Back in Colorado, I was wheeled into the operating room for repair work, this time on my leg. In order to allow some movement in my immobile right foot, the surgeons transferred a tendon in that foot downward, attaching it to the bottom of my foot with an Army overcoat button. The button stayed there for a few months while I healed. For the rest of my life I'd walk with a floppy foot.

After four days back recuperating in my old ward, I returned to the barracks. I was only there a week when I received orders to return to the main hospital for amputation of my left arm.

I held the orders as if they were a grenade that was definitely, without question—well, probably—a dud.

"These sure the hell can't be for me," I said to the sergeant who was occupying the main desk in the barracks. "Somebody fucked up."

"Sure, Myers," the sergeant said, taking the papers and looking them over. "It sure enough has your name there. Don't go chicken-shit on us now. Pack your gear and get over there."

I put on my garrison cap and trudged back to the hospital, trying to manipulate a full length leg cast, a crutch, a heavy duffel bag and a sling-secured arm. On the way to the nursing station, I lectured myself: Be prepared for anything.

The nurse looked up.

"What are you doing here?"

"I've got orders. See?"

I handed her the form.

"Oh, damn. This isn't you, this is supposed to be Mearson."

"Yeah," I said, trying to sound more casual than relieved. "I figured they got something wrong."

"Go back to your barracks, Myers. I'll straighten this out."

I complied, jubilantly, thinking "Mearson, you stupid bastard, you're going to get your arm cut off!"

Rather than needing more surgery, I was recovering well. The pushing and pulling of physical therapy was strengthening my arm and I was getting around more easily with the help of a walking cast. So, in three weeks, the Army transferred me to another tier in its health care system, a wooden barracks on the outskirts of the hospital compound.

In relatively little pain and under less supervision, I settled into a rather enjoyable lifestyle. I still wore the soft blue outfit of a patient rather than a stiff uniform and was given no duty more drudging than policing the nearby grounds with the other patients each morning.

I was given one assignment, though, presumably because of my self-proclaimed artistic experience. Before and after my late morning therapy sessions, I assembled photographic slides for the doctors. Most of the slides were of diseased or wounded limbs and surgical procedures. Most were unpleasant. The worst pictured the remains of a pilot whose jet had exploded on an Air Force runway. The only exceptions to the pathological lot were one doctor's slides of a beautifully posed, beautifully intact, naked woman.

That duty only lasted two weeks. There was plenty of free time and plenty to fill it, thanks to buddies and wheels. Nearly everyone had saved money while in Vietnam. Those bankrolled paychecks found their way into car dealers' hands more often than not. Cars provided status and escape for the patients, who piled into their GTOs, their Camaros, their Mustangs—usually with someone's cast sticking out a window—and went out for steak-and-potato meals and endless beers in endless bars.

I wanted an old Thunderbird. I pored over the classifieds until I found a white one and, with $1,200 and lots of tinkering, acquired a respectable little sports car. It had the advantage of being a two-seater, so I could not be expected to transport my fellow rowdies on their frequent forays into town. I didn't want to accept responsibility for the sometimes-drunken group and didn't want to expose the T-Bird's 1955 upholstery to roughhousing.

The primary vehicle for our group of carousers was a gold Oldsmobile 98 convertible. Six or seven civvies-clad guys, complete with casts and canes, could pile into it. The owner of the Olds was a Chicagoan who had lost a leg when someone threw him onto a grenade. The radio operator for his company command, he had been in a ravine with the officers and a first sergeant when a Chi-com grenade was tossed into it. Although his citation for a Distinguished Service Cross read as if he had voluntarily sacrificed himself to protect the others, he swore that it was the sergeant who threw him on that grenade.

Jerry, the one fraternizing with the physical therapist, was one of my closest friends among the rowdies. Another was a sergeant who was the senior member of the group by virtue of his two-year residency at the hospital. One of his feet had been blown off by a mine. His leg had been amputated at mid-calf, only to become infected, then amputated at the knee, only to become infected again. A third amputation had left a stump that ended at mid thigh and he was waiting to see if he would need more surgery. Yet he was a jovial sort, a gone-to-fat jock who still excelled on Colorado's amputee ski team and enjoyed riding ever-bigger motorcycles on his leaves home to St. Louis.

The sergeant's length of stay at Fitzsimmons was nearly equaled by Matti, the quietest member of the group. Tall and thin, he'd been shot seven times at point-blank range with a machine gun when he walked around a corner in An Khe during the Tet offensive. He and I shared the distinction of having suffered bullet wounds. Everyone else in the barracks who we knew had been shredded by mines, B-40 rockets, grenades, artillery rounds or bombs.

Hornsby, who instigated many of our nighttime adventures, had been hit in the legs by shrapnel. He had a Gary Cooperish rough presence about him, which was heightened by endless tales of his exploits on the battlefield and in bed. At 23 or so, he was a few years older than the rest of us. We wanted to believe in his stories but weren't sure we could. Our first indication that Hornsby wasn't bullshitting came when he told us about a couple who were friends of his.

"You'll have to meet 'em," he said. "They've got a cabin up in the hills. He hunts and fishes every day. His wife is just excruciatingly beautiful. And she likes to walk around the cabin naked."

He offered to take us on a weekend visit to this sylvan Adam and Eve, and we accepted. Even if Hornsby's story was a crock o' crap, the trip could be a hoot. So we hopped into the Oldsmobile and took off on a Friday afternoon. It was dark by the time we pulled up to the cabin.

It was a picturesque, isolated setting. We were greeted by a bearded, earthy fellow behind whom, in the open cabin doorway, stood a beautiful long-haired woman who wore nothing but one of her husband's long flannel shirts. We went inside and watched, flabbergasted, as she moved on naked legs about the cabin, pouring coffee. That night we turned restlessly in our sleeping bags, savoring thoughts of her. The next morning, we chowed down on her pancakes.

After one other episode—this one at a watering hole in Boulder—we believed anything Hornsby said.

It was a Friday night. After horsing around the University of Colorado campus for awhile, we stopped at a dark, seedy, shoebox of a bar. We were in a booth, sipping on our beers, when an attractive woman came in and, without looking around, sat down at the bar. She was in her late 20s, a bit old for us. Hornsby looked at us and smiled.

"Whatta ya wanna bet?" he asked. "You want to bet 10 bucks that she'll pick me up?"

Someone took him up on it, and Hornsby walked to the bar, sat down and ordered a beer. The woman glanced at him from the opposite end of the bar. She turned away, gazing intently at the row of bottles gleaming behind the bartender. Then she looked at Hornsby again. Turned away again. Then she looked at Hornsby a little more before getting up, walking over and sitting next to him. She didn't act familiar with him, as if they'd been together before. But within 15 minutes, she handed him her car keys and they walked arm-in-arm out of the place.

Five pairs of eyes at the booth followed them and five pairs of hands pounded on the table as we roared at Hornsby's conquest.

He didn't show up until Monday morning roll call.

There were other good times that summer. Hooting and hollering in the movies, watching the moon landing from a crowded bar in a tiny mountain town, going to auto races, roaring endlessly down Aurora Boulevard on the way to somewhere interesting.

In August, a military cloud cast a shadow on my idyllic summer. I was summoned to the main hospital, where a civilian secretary handed me some papers.

"Here are all of your orders, transferring you to another barracks," she said with a lipsticked smile. "Don't lose them. They're the only copies."

Another barracks. A full-duty barracks. Going there meant I'd have to wear a uniform again. And salute. And do Christ knew what kind of duty.

I walked slowly down the hospital halls, across the sidewalks and to my bunk, where I stretched out to contemplate my fate.

It didn't seem quite right. In a few weeks I'd be in as good as shape as the Army could get me and I'd be officially retired from the service. I couldn't bear the thought of all that shit-ass routine I'd endured in training. All of that yes-sirring and no-sirring hadn't made me a better soldier, hadn't made me a better shot or a better packhorse on the jungle trails. And it wasn't going to make a damned bit of difference for whatever awaited me in the Real World.

Besides, I was comfortable right where I was, in Barracks 418. I had friends, I had fun. If there was any thorn in my rosy situation, it was the nurse who was in charge of the barracks. He was short, black and muscular in a pudgy sort of way. He also had a practiced feminine way of moving, which he seemed to flaunt, and a habit of constant gossip and badmouthing that once made me explode with "You goddamn stupid fruit, why don't you just knock off that silly shit?" But even the fact that he had it out for me wasn't enough to make me want to move.

I'd already paid my dues.

I sat up in the bunk, crumpled the orders and tossed the paper ball into a wastebasket. Then I got up and threw more trash in on top of it.

That assured me of not having to be a soldier again.

As far as the main hospital was concerned, I was at the new barracks, which didn't even know I existed. I simply stayed on at 418, which had no orders transferring me. I continued therapy and recreation as I had before, only now my days included the added excitement that came with sneaking in to pick up my mail, which was being forwarded to a slot in the full-duty barracks.

In September, a medical board found me officially unfit for further duty because of my wounds. I had enough rotation in my makeshift shoulder joint to make my arm useful. A leg brace attached to my black military shoes had replaced the series of casts and bandages on my badly scarred leg. I had limited movement of my right foot and walked with a slight limp, but my weight was up to 220 and I felt strong, thanks to hours of physical therapy and my scuba diving classes.

In October, my dad flew to Denver to get my Thunderbird. He drove the unheated convertible up the long, cold highways to Boise.

In November, I attended a meeting at which a weary sergeant tried to explain to a roomful of noisy veterans how their percentage of disability was calculated. In my case, a 40 percent leg injury and a 30 percent arm injury added up to 60 percent total disability.

At the start of the meeting, the sergeant reminded us that we, of course, had the opportunity to re-enlist should a medical board re-examination find us fit. His voice was drowned out by hoots before he could finish.

A few days later, I was in the barracks, packing up.

I was alone in a two-bed room that I'd shared for a month by virtue of my assignment to be in charge of the first floor wing. Most of my buddies had been released, making me the senior patient. My only incursion into command had been to manhandle a drunken soldier from bed and carry him back to the john to clean up his vomit, which had been deposited on the old steam radiator.

As I folded and crammed my stuff into my new duffle bag, I thought about the days of intensive living I'd experienced in Vietnam. Compared with that moment-to-moment existence, even the most entertaining moments in Denver had been dull. I was ready for new adventures. I stuck my release papers and airplane ticket into a black AWOL bag.

Then the door flew open. The barracks nurse was standing there, pointing a finger at me. He lisped with some drama, "There he is!" The sergeant was talking to the chief of nurses, who stood next to him. She was a major. She looked like Lucille Ball gone to seed. Her red hair was styled like a helmet above her light green summer uniform, which was studded with gold leaves. She seemed confused but listened intently as the sergeant blathered on. He'd somehow learned about my August orders to transfer, and was determined that Spec. Myers be duly punished for ignoring them.

I was in a mental fog about leaving, and didn't catch all of his words. At any rate, I didn't want to listen to it any more. "Hey, I don't have time for this. I really don't. A guy's out there warming up his car, waiting for me," I said, nodding toward the window. "See? He's warming up his car." They didn't move.

I picked up the AWOL bag and field jacket with one hand and flung the duffle bag over my shoulder with the other. I shoved my way past my dumbfounded superiors.

"Excuse me, pardon me," I said, as if it was an everyday occurrence for Spec. 4's to dismiss sergeants and majors. Instead of whining or groveling or praying to God that they didn't put me in the stockade, I just cut out. Split man. So long, Louie.

I took a shortcut out a side door and hopped into my buddy's jet-black GTO.

"Let's hit it!"

In less than a minute we were past the gate of the hospital compound. I turned to watch the MPs who were guarding it. I smiled with relief as their figures grew smaller and smaller and finally disappeared in the rear view mirror.

Seventeen Months, Twenty-nine Days

Chapter 19: Stay out

I carried paper and pencils with me throughout my Vietnam tour and had quite a humble sketchbook put together. Charlie got all that stuff, I guess. I never saw my rucksack again. What I did bring back to the States was a permanently floppy foot and a shoulder that rarely stopped hurting.

Two years after I left Fitzsimmons, I was a 22-year-old, long-haired Seattle art student. The Army said I should report to McChord Air Force Base for my medical retirement physical. I caught a bus to Tacoma for the two-day process. It included a complete eye exam, something the Army had never bothered to give me.

The eye doc asked me how long I'd had my current eyeglass prescription. I pulled out my wallet and extracted the latest copy, dated 1966. He looked at the creased piece of paper and told me to stay put. Then he left the exam room.

For the next five minutes, I heard mumbling through the closed door. Then the doc came back in with another doctor, and the two laid into me with a passion, saying I needed to sue the government because without my glasses I was legally blind. Too blind, at least, to be drafted.

They were pretty hot about it in an anti-war-protester way.

To get them off my back, I told them I'd think about it. Could an ex-soldier even sue the government? Hell, I doubted it. Would I if I could? I doubted that, too.

I was dead sure about other things. Like the best course of action for Paul Mills, one of my Idaho buddies. He got a low draft number and then passed his Army physical with flying colors. To stay out of Vietnam, he was left debating whether to move to Canada—meaning he might never get to visit his family again—or whether to avoid active duty as a conscientious objector.

Paul asked my advice. I said if he didn't file for CO status, I'd personally drive him to Canada and throw his ass over the border.

When Vice President Spiro Agnew came to Boise, I tagged along with Paul to a protest march at the Red Lion Hotel where Agnew was staying. We were met by the local gendarmes and their German shepherds. Within a year, Agnew, facing tax evasion charges, resigned. A year later, in the wake of the Watergate scandal, our rough 'n' ready Commander in Chief Richard Nixon also called it quits.

And the year after that, in 1975, the Vietnam War was over.

Epilogue: Grady C. Myers, 1949-2011

Grady Curtis Myers – artist, decorated combat veteran, car aficionado, storyteller and most of all loving father – died July 30, 2011, in Boise, Idaho. He was 61.

Grady was born Oct. 6, 1949, in Roswell, New Mexico. He was the son of O.V. "Zeke" Myers and Mary Thornton Myers. He grew up in an Air Force family, and moved frequently as a child.

The family eventually settled in Boise, where Grady graduated from Borah High School in 1967. He served with the U.S. Army's 4th Infantry Division during the Vietnam War, and was awarded the Purple Heart for wounds suffered during a 1969 ambush in the Plei Trap Valley.

Grady attended Boise State College and the Burnley School for Professional Art in Seattle. He went on to a career as a newspaper artist with The Idaho Statesman in Boise and The Spokesman-Review in Spokane, Washington. He later worked as a graphic information specialist for the Idaho Panhandle National Forests in Coeur d'Alene.

His artistic accomplishments ranged from decorations on his squad's combat helmets to a tourist map of Boise; from historic signs along North Idaho's Route of the Hiawatha trail to T-shirts for the Bare Buns Fun Run. His work is included in the collection of the National Veterans Art Museum in Chicago.

Grady was known for his enthusiasm for classic automobiles, especially those in need of rescue and ongoing attention.

Grady was married to Rayleen Burgess, then Julie Titone. Both marriages ended in divorce.

He is survived by a son and daughter-in-law, Jake Liam Myers and Sarah Myers; a daughter, Mary Megan Myers; stepson Kevin Myers; stepson and daughter-in-law John and Helen Myers; granddaughter Alexandra Myers and step-granddaughters Emily Myers and Mariah Frank. He was preceded in death by his parents and his brother, Ken Myers.

Made in the USA
Lexington, KY
17 July 2014